THE GREAT INTERNATIONAL BARBECUE BOOK

Books by Myra Waldo include:

Casserole Cookbook

Complete Round the World Cookbook

Myra Waldo's Chinese Cookbook

Myra Waldo's Dessert Cookbook

Myra Waldo's Restaurant Guide to New York City and Vicinity

Myra Waldo's Travel and Motoring Guide to Europe

Myra Waldo's Travel Guide to the Orient and the Pacific

Myra Waldo's Travel Guide to South America

THE GREAT INTERNATIONAL BARBECUE BOOK

by Myra Waldo

McGRAW-HILL BOOK COMPANY

New York   St. Louis   San Francisco   Bogotá   Guatemala
Hamburg   Lisbon   Madrid   Mexico   Montreal   Panama
Paris   San Juan   São Paulo   Tokyo   Toronto

First paperback edition, 1981

2 3 4 5 6 7 8 9 0 FGFG 8 7 6 5 4 3 2 1

Library of Congress Cataloging in Publication Data

Waldo, Myra.
The great international barbecue book.

Includes index.
Barbecue cookery.   2. Cookery, International.
I. Title.
TX840.B3W33   641.7′6   78-8654
ISBN 0-07-067777-8
0-07-067778-6 (paperback)

Contents

Introduction

I TRAVEL around the world constantly, averaging about
a quarter-million miles each year. Sometimes I think I am
more comfortable aboard a jet plane than in my own home.
While traveling, I invariably eat the food of the country in
which I find myself. I have been very much impressed that
almost every nation has a number of extremely ingenious and
unique recipes for preparing food over open fires. After many
years I have compiled these recipes into the first and only
international barbecue cookbook. All previously published

barbecue books are basically American-style: plain meat, poultry, or fish is cooked over an open, usually charcoal-burning fire, and a limited number of sauces or marinades is suggested.

The Great International Barbecue Book includes the best and most interesting recipes from all over the globe. For example, Korean Sesame Pork is quite delicious, although unknown to most Americans. Chicken Tandoor, that exquisite creation from India, is rarely served in our country although it is quite easy to prepare. From the South Pacific comes an entire series of barbecue recipes in which the flavor of the foods is completely retained during the cooking process by wrapping in foil.

How did barbecuing start? What are its origins?

Thousands of years ago a hunter returned from the forest, dragging the carcass of a wild animal. Flinging it down, he graciously accepted the plaudits of his mate and offspring.

Then the hunter built a large fire in the family cave, cut great chunks of meat, and placed them over the roaring blaze. As flames leaped high, the meat sizzled until the great man indicated that it was ready. The family took flint knives and cut off giant-sized pieces; then they groaned in unison.

The Mighty Hunter had done it again! The meat was black and burned on the outside, uncooked inside. Patiently, the woman took another slab of meat and cooked it properly over the concentrated heat of glowing embers.

Today, many men are still burning meats over outdoor fires, but others are masterful outdoor chefs. A man who couldn't be persuaded, under any circumstances, to help in the kitchen, much less to cook, presides proudly over his charcoal fire. Although hundreds of centuries have gone by, the hunter-and-provider-of-food instinct remains. A basic, perhaps primitive, urge makes men enjoy performing this type of cookery.

Man first had the necessity, then the desire to cook over open fires. The Roman legions—determined to conquer the Western world—cooked over blazing logs in their temporary camps. Ancient Persians grilled meats over smaller braziers. They're still doing it. *Shish kabobs* originated somewhere in the Middle East, although no one knows the precise spot. In Turkish, *shish* means sword, and *kabob* is broiled meat; thus *shish kabob* is literally meat on a skewer. Nomadic Mideastern people camped out at night, slaughtered an animal, and skewered cubes of meat on a sword which they held over an open fire. On the steppes of Russia the Tatars cooked lamb, and the *shashlik* has a meaning similar to *shish kabob.*

During the eleventh century Genghis Khan and his hordes swept across China. They ate whatever and whenever they could, roasting various foods over an open fire—a style of cookery that is still popular in northern China. In medieval times every castle had an enormous roasting spit, on which whole cattle were barbecued, while balladeers sang rondels of love to dainty maidens. Later those same maidens ate pounds of meat at a sitting, scattering bones on the floor.

In the Southern United States, during the last century, barbecues became traditional forms of hospitality, with everyone invited. In order to attract voters, Southern politicians scheduled series of barbecues, county by county. There was a regular pattern to these political feasts—a loud brass band, pretty girls, and all the liquor and barbecued meat that anyone could consume, plus a boring speech by a would-be officeholder. Everyone, in the name of good manners, was required to put up with the speech in exchange for the food.

Nowadays the family barbecue is at the peak of popularity. But why is it called "barbecue"—a strange word, when you think about it? There are two theories. One is that it originated with the Caribbean pirates who came ashore, built a fire hastily, and roasted any available animal *barbe à queue,* that is, from head to tail. Others believe it is a modification of the Spanish word *barbacoa,* a word used to describe a frame from which meats were suspended. Whatever the theory, barbecuing is now part of the English—or is it American?—language.

There are comparatively few countries around the world that do not practice outdoor grilling, barbecuing, or smoke cookery. In the Scandinavian countries smoke cooking is a regular way of life. In India, Indonesia, China, Greece, and Persia (now Iran) it is still customary to cook in barbecue fashion.

The recipes in this book represent the best of outdoor barbecue cooking, although many of the recipes lend themselves very well to indoor use.

Happy barbecuing!

Myra Waldo

SOME SUBSTITUTIONS

Almost every town and city has a supermarket or ethnic store where herbs and spices used in the recipes in this book are available. However, there may not be an Oriental or Asiatic food shop in your particular community, and for that reason, a list of possible substitutes are given below.

Chinese black beans: Soak ¼ cup of dried black beans overnight in water to cover. Drain, cover with fresh water and cook 30 minutes. Drain. Mix the beans with 2 teaspoons salt, let stand overnight at room temperature, and use as directed. The beans will have a slightly fermented taste.

Chinese sesame oil: Use the amount of regular sesame oil specified in the recipe, and add ⅛ teaspoon of Tabasco.

Chinese Five-Spice Powder: Combine equal amounts of cinnamon, ground cloves, powdered ginger, and nutmeg.

Ginger Root: Any of the following are suggested. Ginger in syrup, rinsed thoroughly in cold water; canned or bottled ginger; candied ginger, rinsed carefully of all sugar.

Hoisin Sauce: Combine ½ cup of puréed plum jam, 2 cloves minced garlic, ⅛ teaspoon Tabasco, and ½ teaspoon beef extract.

THE GREAT INTERNATIONAL BARBECUE BOOK

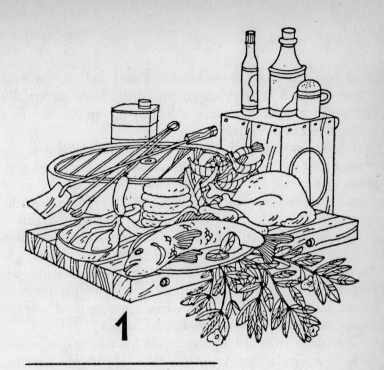

1

Equipment

BARBECUING EQUIPMENT can be as simple as a disposable aluminum-foil grill intended to be used only once, or it may be as magnificent as a covered grill with side tables for carving. There are grills intended to be used with charcoal or specially prepared briquets. Others are made for use with ceramic tiles or permanent volcanic briquets; these are heated by electricity, which produces the necessary heat buildup that results in the true charcoal flavor but eliminates the need for cleaning up the charcoal ash. Still other grills use volcanic rocks with gas tanks as the source of fuel and also produce a true charcoal taste. Many of the grills have electrically operated rotisseries; some are battery-driven for locations without electrical outlets.

Smoke cooking has become very popular, and almost any regular grill can be used for this purpose. As a rule, hickory chips or powder are used. For best results, soak the wood chips in water for a half hour and distribute them over the source of heat. The food will develop a delightful smoky flavor. (However, don't overdo the amount of smoke.) There are also special water smokers, which use a pan of water in the grill to keep the foods moist during the smoking process. In some parts of the country, dried corncobs are used instead of wood. For a novelty, all-bran cereals may be used over the source of heat to produce a delicious taste.

Fireplace grills are also available for indoor use, where there is a satisfactory draft. For tableside indoor cooking, small hibachis are practical and easy to use.

The following is a list (in alphabetical order) of manufacturers and the types of grills available:

BIG BOY

Small, picnic-size (charcoal) grills with a crankup grill.
Portable large grills on wheels, also with crankup grill.
Rotisserie grills, both electrically operated and cordless (battery-driven).
Steak wagon grills on wheels.
Covered cookers with adjustable grills.
Smoke wagons.
Charcoal water smokers.

BUDDY L GRILLS

Square grills for use with charcoal.
Covered grills.

Square smokers.
Covered charcoal wagons on wheels.
Smoker wagons.
Portable smoker wagons with cordless motors for rotisserie.
Kettle grills.
Brazier-type grills.
Tabletop electric grills (using volcanic briquets).
Hibachis.

CHAR-B-QUE

Covered electric grills using permanent lava rock, mostly small sizes suitable for steaks, chops, and kabobs.

CHAR-O

Tabletop grills.
Charcoal smokers.

CRESTLINE

Tabletop and pedestal-based hibachis.
Smoke grills on stands with wheels.
Brazier grills with snap-on hoods.
Gas grills for use with lava rock.
Electric grills.
Wagon grills.

MECCO

Charcoal grills.
Smoker grills with rotisserie.
Porcelain grills with smoker.
Porcelain gas cookers using volcanic rocks.

SMOKE 'N PIT

Pit smokers
Charcoal and water.
Electrically driven.
Double Smoke 'N Stack.

WEBER

Charcoal barbecue kettle with collapsible features that
make it portable.
Sequoia wagon: kettle in a redwood wagon.
Ranch: large kettle on wheels.
Electric barbecue kettles: use volcanic rock.
Gas barbecuing kettles: for use with natural or liquid
petroleum.

MOST OF THE MANUFACTURERS offer a number of acces-
sories that are quite helpful for better barbecuing. These
include:

Asbestos gloves.
Double-hinged wire grills and baskets.
Spit forks.
Long-handled tongs, forks, and turners.
Aluminum drip pans.
Kabob skewers.
Charcoal electric lighters.
Spit sets (complete kits).
Hickory (or other wood) chips and powders.

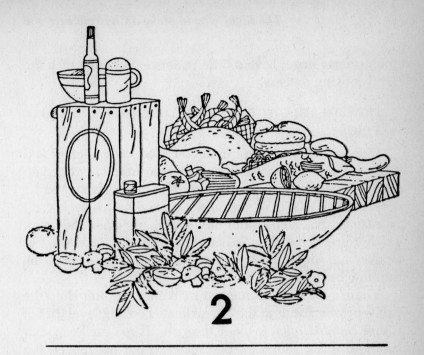

2

The Right Way to Make a Charcoal Fire

GETTING THE FIRE STARTED

1. Stack the charcoal or briquets into a mound or pyramid, permitting the air to circulate through them.
2. Use a starter such as one of the electric types, or a liquid starter will work. Be sure the grill is sheltered from the wind when using a liquid starter.
3. Allow about half an hour for the fire to reach its

proper stage; have a little patience and don't rush the cooking process.

HOW TO TELL THE TEMPERATURE OF A CHARCOAL FIRE

Charcoal briquets vary from one product to another and some are ready for cooking sooner than others, but certain general rules prevail. During the day, the coals should be covered with a layer of gray ashes. At night, this layer won't be easy to spot, so consider the coals ready when they emit a rather bright red glow. When they are ready, take tongs or a poker and spread the coals out into a close single layer. You can now begin to cook.

There's a tried-and-true test for a charcoal fire. Hold the palms of your hands at the approximate cooking level (but of course be certain not to touch the grill). If you can keep your hands in this position for two seconds, but not longer, the fire is hot and ready to cook. (It may also, on occasion, be *too* hot.) If you can hold your palms for three seconds, the fire is medium-hot; for four seconds, medium. If you can keep your palms in that position for five seconds or more, the fire is probably too cool for cooking.

To raise the temperature, use a poker to gently tap away the ashes from the charcoal; then push them closer together.

To lower the temperature, separate the coals with a poker, or raise the grid.

HOW TO MAKE THE CLEANING-UP JOB ALL THE EASIER

There are spray products which give the grill a special antisticking coating; follow the instructions on the can.

If there is a substantial accumulation of grease or food particles, sprinkle dry baking soda on a damp sponge and scour. Then rinse with a solution of baking soda and water.

After each use, the grill should be cleaned and then covered.

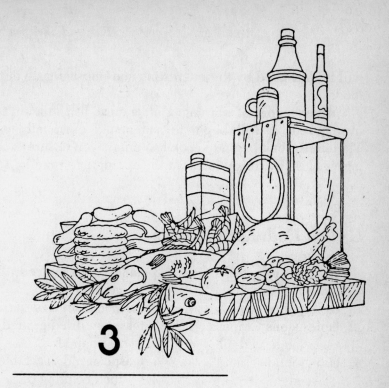

3

Fish and Shellfish

BARBECUING ORDINARILY brings to mind the use of meat. However, fish and shellfish are novel additions to the standard foods used in barbecuing and are especially delicious when prepared with the use of marinades and sauces before grilling. Although specific kinds of fish are indicated in the recipes, any firm-fleshed fish available in your area may be used. When fish or shellfish are prepared over a barbecue, everyone will be intrigued by the interesting and unusual taste of the food.

Just one word of warning: Unlike meat, fish shouldn't be overcooked; it will begin to soften and even fall apart. Therefore, don't begin to cook fish unless you're sure everyone is close by, ready to eat at the appropriate time.

Grilled Cod, Korean Style

6 small codfish steaks	3 tablespoons minced green onion
¾ cup soy sauce	
3 tablespoons sugar	2 teaspoons minced garlic
2 tablespoons Chinese sesame-seed oil	⅛ teaspoon dried ground red pepper
¼ cup ground sesame seeds	¼ teaspoon red vegetable food coloring

Rinse and dry the fish. Mix all remaining ingredients. Dip fish in mixture, coating both sides.

Arrange on greased rack, 4 inches over heat. Grill 15 minutes, basting with mixture and turning several times.

Serves 6.

Barbecued Fish, Southern Style

1 4-pound striped bass or similar fish	½ teaspoon freshly ground black pepper
1 cup cider vinegar	½ cup grated onion
1 cup tomato sauce	2 cloves garlic, minced
2 teaspoons salt	1 teaspoon thyme

Remove the head of the fish; clean, rinse, and dry.

Mix all remaining ingredients in a bowl. Put the fish in the mixture and baste well to coat. Cover and marinate in refrigerator overnight. Baste several times. Drain, reserving the marinade.

Put fish on a greased double-hinged wire grill 5 inches over the heat. Grill 30 minutes, basting with some of the reserved marinade and turning several times. Heat the remaining marinade, and serve as a sauce.

Serves 4–6.

Grilled Fish, Greek Style

2 3-pound mackerel, striped bass, or similar fish
½ cup olive oil
½ cup lemon juice
2 teaspoons salt
½ teaspoon freshly ground black pepper
½ teaspoon crumbled rosemary
2 tablespoons minced parsley
Greek olives

Remove the heads of the fish; clean, wash, and dry.

In a shallow oblong dish, mix all remaining ingredients. Marinate fish in mixture 1 hour, basting frequently. Drain.

Place the fish in a greased double-hinged wire grill. Place fish 5 inches over the heat and grill 30 minutes, turning and basting with marinade several times. Serve with Greek olives.

Serves 6–8.

Grilled Fish, Indian Style

6 slices fish, 1½ inches
   thick
2 teaspoons salt
¾ teaspoon freshly ground
   black pepper
¼ teaspoon ground cloves
1 teaspoon ground
   coriander seeds

½ teaspoon ground ginger
¾ cup yogurt
6 1½-inch-thick slices
   onion
4 tablespoons melted
   butter

Wash and dry the fish. Mix salt, pepper, cloves, coriander, ginger, and yogurt. Spread over both sides of the fish. Let stand 30 minutes. Put an onion slice on each piece of fish and secure with small skewer.

Arrange fish on a greased double-hinged wire grill 5 inches over heat. Grill 25 minutes, turning and basting several times with the butter.

Serves 6.

Sweet and Sour Fish, Fijian Style

6 slices striped bass,
   1 inch thick
¼ cup cider vinegar
½ cup vegetable oil
3 tablespoons soy sauce

2 tablespoons dry sherry
2 tablespoons sugar
2 teaspoons minced ginger
   root
½ cup crushed pineapple

Rinse and dry the fish. Mix all remaining ingredients. Marinate fish in the mixture for 1 hour, turning frequently. Drain; pour marinade into a saucepan.

Arrange fish on a greased double-hinged wire grill 5

inches over heat, turning several times. While the fish is cooking, bring the marinade to a boil and cook over low heat for 5 minutes. Serve in a sauceboat.

Serves 6.

Walnut-Stuffed Fish, Jordanian Style

4 pounds whole striped
    bass or similar fish
¾ cup olive oil
3 teaspoons salt
1½ teaspoons freshly
    ground black pepper
1 cup chopped onions

1½ cups finely chopped
    green pepper
1 cup coarsely chopped
    walnuts
½ cup chopped parsley
Lemon slices

If preferred, remove the head of the fish. Split and bone fish for stuffing. Wash and dry the fish. Rub inside and out with ¼ cup of oil, and sprinkle with 2 teaspoons of salt and half the pepper. Let stand while preparing stuffing.

Heat remaining oil in a skillet; sauté the onions for 5 minutes. Add green peppers and sauté for 5 minutes, stirring frequently. Stir in walnuts, and sauté 5 minutes longer. Remove from heat and mix in parsley and remaining salt and pepper. Stuff the fish, and close the opening with skewers or sew it.

Cut a piece of heavy-duty aluminum foil large enough to completely enfold the fish. Put fish in the center and fold up the foil, sealing the edges well. Place on a grill 5 inches over heat and grill 1 hour, turning the package several times. Unfold foil and carefully transfer fish to a platter. Garnish with lemon slices.

Serves 4.

African Lobster Tails

12 frozen lobster tails
1 cup dry vermouth
¼ cup lemon juice

1½ teaspoons salt
⅛ teaspoon Tabasco
½ cup melted butter

Thaw lobster tails and cut through the shells as package directs. Mix vermouth, lemon juice, salt, and Tabasco. Put the lobster tails in the mixture shell side up, and let stand 30 minutes, basting and turning several times.

Drain lobster tails and place them on a greased double-hinged wire grill 5 inches over the heat. Grill 4 minutes, shell side up, then turn over, baste with some of the marinade and melted butter, and grill 10 minutes longer, basting frequently. Test the meat by making a small cut in it—it should look opaque. If not, cook a little longer. Serve with additional melted butter.

Serves 4–6.

Barbecued Mackerel, Yugoslavian Style

2 2-pound mackerel
2 teaspoons salt
1 teaspoon freshly ground
    black pepper

Bay leaves
Olive oil
Lemon juice
Chopped parsley

Have fish cut into slices 1 inch thick. Season with the salt and pepper. Using 6 skewers, thread fish on skewers, alternating each slice with a bay leaf. Place 4 inches over heat and grill 15 minutes. Baste frequently with olive oil and lemon juice, and turn skewers until both sides are brown. Serve sprinkled with parsley.

Serves 6.

Tasmanian Scallops

24 sea scallops
Salt
White pepper

18 cherry tomatoes
¼ cup dry white wine
¼ cup melted butter

Wash and dry the scallops. Sprinkle each with salt and pepper. Using 6 skewers, thread scallops and tomatoes onto them, starting and ending with the scallops. Brush all over with a mixture of wine and butter. Broil 4 inches over the heat, about 7 minutes. Baste frequently with the wine mixture and turn the skewers several times.

Serves 6.

Broiled Shrimp, Thai Style

2 pounds large raw shrimp
¼ cup sesame-seed or
   peanut oil
¼ cup lemon juice
2 teaspoons salt
¼ teaspoon dried ground
   red pepper

2 cloves garlic, minced
1 teaspoon ground cumin
   seeds
1 teaspoon ground
   coriander seeds
1 teaspoon ground ginger

Wash, shell, and devein the shrimp. Mix all remaining ingredients. Marinate the shrimp in the mixture for 2 hours at room temperature. Drain, reserving the marinade.

Arrange the shrimp on a greased close-mesh double-hinged wire grill. Place 5 inches from the heat. Grill 10 minutes, turning and basting with the marinade several times.

Serves 6–8.

Lemon Shrimp, New Zealand Style

2 pounds raw shrimp,
    shelled and deveined
¼ pound (1 stick) butter
¼ cup lemon juice

3 tablespoons
    Worcestershire
    sauce

Wash and dry the shrimp. Melt butter, and stir in lemon juice and Worcestershire sauce. Marinate shrimp in the mixture for 2 hours. Drain the shrimp and arrange on a greased close-meshed double-hinged wire grill. Broil 5 minutes, turning the rack and basting with the lemon mixture. Pierce with cocktail picks to serve as an hors d'oeuvre, or serve as a first course.

Serves 4–6.

Swordfish, Hawaiian Style

3 pounds swordfish, or
    other firm-fleshed
    fish, 1 inch thick
½ cup pineapple juice
2 tablespoons lemon juice
¼ cup soy sauce
2 tablespoons chili sauce

1 teaspoon minced garlic
1 teaspoon salt
¾ teaspoon freshly ground
    black pepper
2 tablespoons minced
    parsley

Wash and dry the fish; cut into 6 pieces. In a glass or pottery bowl or baking pan, mix all remaining ingredients. Marinate the fish in the mixture for 2 hours, turning several times.

When ready to cook, drain fish, reserving the marinade. Arrange fish on a greased double-hinged wire grill 4 inches over the heat, and put a drip pan under it. Grill 10 minutes, turning and basting several times. Transfer to serving dish.

Pour drippings from drip pan into a saucepan and add any remaining marinade. Bring to a boil and pour over the fish.

Serves 6.

German Grilled Trout

6 brook trout	1 teaspoon grated lemon
2 teaspoons salt	rind
¾ teaspoon freshly ground	8 bay leaves
black pepper	½ cup melted butter
1 cup dry white wine	Lemon quarters
¼ cup lemon juice	Grilled tomatoes

If the trout are frozen, thaw. Rinse and dry the fish, removing the heads if you like. Cut 3 shallow gashes on each side of the fish. Rub fish with the salt and pepper, and arrange side by side in an oblong pan or dish.

Mix wine, lemon juice, and rind. Pour the mixture over fish and let marinate for 2 hours, turning a few times.

Use a double-hinged wire grill and spread the bay leaves over one side. Drain the trout and arrange over the bay leaves. Brush top with melted butter. Close the grill, and place it 5 inches over heat.

Grill 20 minutes; turn rack several times and baste the fish with melted butter. Discard bay leaves. Serve fish with lemon quarters and grilled tomatoes.

Serves 6–12.

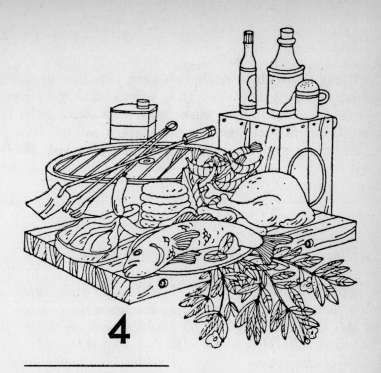

4

Poultry

MOST POULTRY—but particularly chicken—tends to be somewhat bland in flavor. The recipes for poultry in this section, collected from all over the world, provide unusual and surprising flavors to the expected (and somewhat routine) taste of chicken, for example. The preparation of the chicken (or other bird) should be done ahead of time, as specified in the recipes. Then grill in the usual fashion. Game birds, duck, and goose all lend themselves to barbecuing, although chicken is the most popular.

One thought about poultry cooking: it is best to place poultry on a comparatively high level away from the source of heat, because birds are best cooked somewhat slowly. If placed close to very high heat, the chicken will be charred on the outside while the interior will remain partly uncooked. Grill until thickest parts are fork-tender and drumstick meat is soft to touch.

Barbecued Chicken, Indonesian Style

2 4-pound roasting chickens, quartered	1 tablespoon dry mustard
2 teaspoons salt	1 tablespoon brown sugar
½ teaspoon freshly ground black pepper	2 tablespoons soy sauce
¼ cup peanut or vegetable oil	¼ cup cider vinegar
1 cup chopped onions	2 tablespoons lemon juice
2 cloves garlic, minced	1 teaspoon ground ginger
1 cup canned tomato sauce	1 teaspoon ground cumin seed
	½ cup hot water

Wash and dry the chicken. Season with salt and pepper and let stand while preparing sauce.

Heat oil in a saucepan; sauté onions and garlic 5 minutes. Mix in remaining ingredients. Bring to a boil and cook over low heat 15 minutes.

Arrange chicken on a greased double-hinged wire grill 6 inches over heat with drip pan underneath. Brush with some sauce. Close grill cover and cook 45 minutes, turning and brushing with sauce several times. Serve, pouring over chicken any remaining sauce.

Serves 8.

Barbecued Chicken Legs, Korean Style

¼ cup sesame seeds
12 chicken legs
¾ cup soy sauce
3 tablespoons sugar
2 tablespoons grated
 ginger root

⅛ teaspoon Tabasco
3 tablespoons dry white
 wine
¼ cup vegetable oil

In a dry skillet, lightly brown sesame seeds. Set aside. Wash and dry the chicken legs. Combine the soy sauce, sugar, ginger, Tabasco, and wine in a glass or pottery bowl. Marinate legs in the mixture overnight in the refrigerator, or for at least 2 hours at room temperature. Drain and brush with oil.

Arrange the legs on a greased rack 5 inches over the heat. Grill 25 to 35 minutes, turning and brushing with the oil frequently. Serve sprinkled with toasted sesame seeds.

Serves 12.

Barbecued Chicken, Texas Style

2 2–3-pound broiling
 chickens, quartered
¾ cup lemon juice
½ cup vegetable oil
3 tablespoons sugar

2 teaspoons salt
1 teaspoon Tabasco
1 tablespoon
 Worcestershire
 sauce

Wash and dry the chicken. Bring all remaining ingredients to a boil. Pour over the chickens, and let stand 1 hour. Drain, reserving marinade. Arrange chicken quarters on a greased rack 5 inches above heat. Grill 30 minutes, turning several times and brushing with marinade.

Serves 4–8.

Bohemian Chicken

2 2½-pound broilers, quartered
½ cup chili sauce
4 tablespoons cider vinegar
1 teaspoon salt
½ teaspoon freshly ground black pepper
2 teaspoons Worcestershire sauce
½ teaspoon dry mustard
1 clove garlic, minced
4 tablespoons vegetable oil
1 cup minced onions

Wash and dry the chicken. Combine remaining ingredients and marinate chickens in it for 1 hour. Remove chickens from marinade and place on a greased double-hinged wire grill. Grill 5 inches over heat for 20 minutes; turn over and broil 25 minutes longer, basting several times.

Serves 4–8.

Ecuador Orange Chicken

4 whole chicken breasts
2 teaspoons salt
½ teaspoon freshly ground black pepper
2 cups orange juice
2 tablespoons sugar
1 cup minced onion
1 bay leaf, crumbled
¼ teaspoon dried ground red pepper
¼ cup melted butter
Sliced oranges

Cut the chicken breasts in half through the breastbone. Season with salt and pepper.

In a glass or pottery bowl, mix orange juice, sugar, onions, bay leaf, and red pepper. Marinate chicken in the mixture overnight, basting several times. Drain, and reserve marinade.

Brush chicken with butter. Arrange on a greased grill 6 inches over heat. Grill 30 minutes, turning and basting frequently with marinade. Garnish with sliced oranges.
Serves 4–8.

Grilled Chicken, African Style

2 2–3-pound broiling chickens, quartered	Oil
2½ teaspoons salt	1½ cups peanut butter
¾ teaspoon freshly ground black pepper	

Wash and dry the chickens. Season with salt and pepper. Place a piece of aluminum foil large enough to hold the chickens in a layer on a rack 5 inches over the heat. Prick the foil in several places, and brush with oil. Arrange the chicken quarters on it, skin side down. Grill 20 minutes, then turn skin side up and spread peanut butter over skin. Grill 30 minutes longer.
Serves 4–8.

Grilled Lime Chicken, Chilean Style

2 2–3-pound broiling chickens, quartered	1 teaspoon tarragon
½ cup lime or lemon juice	2 teaspoons salt
½ cup vegetable oil	¼ teaspoon Tabasco
2 tablespoons minced onion	

Wash and dry the chicken quarters. Mix all remaining ingredients in a bowl. Marinate the chickens in the mixture for 2 hours. Drain, reserving marinade.

Cut a piece of aluminum foil large enough to hold the chicken in a single layer. Prick the foil, and place on a rack 4 inches over the heat. Arrange chicken on it.

Grill 15 minutes on each side, basting chicken with marinade several times.

Serves 6–8.

Grilled Chicken with Almonds, Indian Style

2 2–3-pound broiling
   chickens, quartered
1½ cups chopped onion
12 cloves garlic, minced
2 tablespoons ground
   coriander seeds
¼ teaspoon saffron

⅓ cup lemon juice
1 cup yogurt
⌄ cup heavy cream
1 cup ground blanched
   almonds
¼ cup melted butter
2 teaspoons salt

Wash and dry chickens. Pound onions, garlic, coriander, saffron, and lemon juice to a paste. Rub chickens with the mixture, covering all sides. Let stand 1 hour.

Squeeze yogurt through cheesecloth to remove as much liquid as possible. Mix the drained yogurt with the cream, almonds, and melted butter. Brush over chickens.

Arrange chicken quarters on a greased double-hinged wire grill 6 inches over the heat. Put a drip pan under it. Grill 45 minutes, or until tender, turning and basting frequently with the cream-nut mixture. Sprinkle with salt before serving.

Serves 4–8.

Grilled Chicken, Hungarian Style

2 2–3-pound broiling
   chickens, quartered
2 teaspoons salt
½ teaspoon freshly ground
   black pepper
1 egg, beaten

½ cup vegetable oil
1 cup red wine vinegar
2 tablespoons grated onion
½ cup sour cream
2 tablespoons paprika

Wash and dry the chicken. Season with salt and pepper and let stand 30 minutes. Mix egg, oil, vinegar, and onion and dip chicken quarters in the mixture. Arrange on a greased rack, skin side up, 4 inches above the heat wtih drip pan underneath. Cook 45 minutes, turning chicken every 10 minutes, and brushing with marinade. After 35 minutes, turn skin side up, and brush with mixture of sour cream and paprika. Cook 10 minutes longer.

Serves 4–8.

Grilled Chicken, Iranian Style

2 2–3-pound broiling
   chickens, quartered
2 teaspoons salt
1 cup grated onions

½ cup lemon juice
¼ cup melted butter
¼ teaspoon ground saffron

Wash and dry chicken. In a glass or pottery bowl, mix salt, onions, and lemon juice. Marinate chicken in the mixture for 2 hours at room temperature. Turn several times to coat the pieces. Drain, reserving the marinade.

Arrange the chicken on a greased double-hinged wire grill. Mix butter and saffron, and brush the chicken with the mixture. Place chicken 5 inches over the heat. Grill 40 minutes, or until tender, turning and basting several times with a mixture of marinade and saffron butter.

Serves 4–8.

Lemon Chicken, Chinese Style

CHICKEN

4	whole chicken breasts	1	tablespoon peanut or vegetable oil
¼	cup soy sauce		
1	tablespoon dry sherry	1	teaspoon salt
2	tablespoons cornstarch	½	teaspoon freshly ground black pepper
1	egg yolk, beaten		

Cut the chicken breasts in half through the breastbone. Remove the skin and bones. Wash and dry the breast meat. Mix all remaining ingredients. Add chicken breasts and let marinate 30 minutes, basting frequently. Arrange the breasts on greased rack and place the rack 4 inches above the heat. Broil 15 to 20 minutes on each side. Meanwhile, prepare the sauce.

SAUCE

3	tablespoons Chinese salted black beans		Salt
2	tablespoons water	4	teaspoons cornstarch
½	cup lemon juice	¼	cup peanut or vegetable oil
1	cup chicken broth		
⅓	cup sugar	1	tablespoon minced garlic
2	tablespoons Chinese sesame-seed oil	½	teaspoon crushed red pepper flakes

Rinse the black beans, then crush with fork. Mix in water and let stand. Mix the lemon juice, broth, sugar, sesame-seed oil, salt, and cornstarch in a bowl. Heat half the oil in a saucepan; stir in garlic for 1 minute. Add lemon mixture and bring to a boil, stirring constantly. Add the black beans and pepper flakes. Cook until clear and thickened. Stir in remaining oil.

Arrange chicken breasts on a heated serving dish and pour the sauce over them, coating each piece well.

Serves 8.

Grilled Chicken, Singapore Style

2 2–3-pound broiling chickens, quartered	1 clove garlic, minced
⅔ cup soy sauce	⅓ cup dry sherry
½ cup vegetable oil	⅓ cup honey
½ cup finely chopped onions	½ teaspoon ground ginger
	¼ cup packaged flaked coconut

Wash and dry the chickens. Mix all remaining ingredients in a bowl. Marinate chickens in the mixture for 2 hours, turning several times.

Drain chicken, reserving the marinade. Arrange chicken, skin side up, on a greased rack with drip pan underneath. Grill for 20 minutes, 6 inches over heat, basting frequently. Turn the chicken over and continue broiling 15 minutes longer, basting frequently with some of the marinade.

Serves 6–8.

Grilled Chicken, Korean Style

2 2–3-pound broiling
 chickens, split
¾ cup soy sauce
1 tablespoon minced garlic
1 tablespoon minced
 ginger root
¾ cup minced scallions

¼ cup ground sesame
 seeds
½ teaspoon dried ground
 red pepper
2 tablespoons Chinese
 sesame-seed oil

Wash and dry the chickens. Mix all remaining ingredients except the sesame-seed oil. Brush mixture on both sides of the chicken and let stand 1 hour. Drain, reserving the marinade.

Put the chicken on a greased rack 6 inches over heat and grill 45 minutes (or until tender), basting and turning frequently. Brush with sesame-seed oil and cook an additional 2 minutes on each side.

Serves 4–8.

Orange Chicken, Israeli Style

3 whole chicken breasts
2 teaspoons salt
1 tablespoon Kitchen
 Bouquet or Gravy
 Master

1 6-ounce can frozen
 orange juice, thawed
½ teaspoon powdered
 ginger
 Orange slices

Cut the chicken breasts through the breastbone. Wash and dry; season with the salt.

Mix the orange juice, Kitchen Bouquet or Gravy Master,

and ginger. Brush the breasts with the mixture. Arrange the chicken on a greased grill, 6 inches over the heat. Cook 25 to 30 minutes, turning and basting with the orange mixture several times. Garnish with orange slices.

Serves 6.

Pakistan Chicken Tikka

2 2½–3-pound broiling chickens, quartered	2 teaspoons cumin seed, crushed
2 cups yogurt	½ teaspoon cayenne pepper
¼ cup lemon juice	
4 drops red vegetable food coloring (optional)	2 teaspoons salt
	¼ cup vegetable oil
3 cloves garlic, minced	Sliced tomatoes
1½ teaspoons grated ginger root	Onion rings
	Lemon wedges

Wash and dry the chicken quarters. Make gashes with a sharp knife along about every inch of meat.

Put the yogurt in a bowl; blend in lemon juice and optional coloring, then garlic, ginger, cumin seed, cayenne, and salt. Add the chicken and turn several times to coat all sides. Let stand 3 hours, turning occasionally.

Remove the quarters and place on double-hinged wire grill. Brush with oil, close the rack, and place about 5 inches over the heat. Grill 10 minutes on each side, or until chicken is tender. Serve with sliced tomatoes, onion rings, and lemon wedges.

Serves 4–8.

Perigord Chicken Breasts

2 whole breasts of chicken
1½ teaspoons salt
½ teaspoon freshly ground
    black pepper
1 4-ounce can pâté de foie
    gras

4 thin slices proscuitto
    ham
¼ cup melted butter
½ cup dry white wine
½ teaspoon crumbled
    tarragon

Cut the breasts in half through the breastbone. Gently loosen the chicken skin but don't remove it. Season with salt and pepper.

Mash the foie gras and stuff it under the loosened chicken skin. Wrap a piece of ham around each breast and secure with a metal skewer. Place a piece of aluminum foil large enough to hold the breasts on a rack 4 inches over the heat. Prick several times. Brush the foil with a little melted butter. Arrange the breasts on the foil.

Grill 15 to 20 minutes on each side, basting frequently with a mixture of wine, tarragon, and remaining butter.

Serves 4.

Thai Sesame Chicken Wings

18 chicken wings
2 tablespoons Chinese
    salted black beans,
    crushed
2 tablespoons water
2 teaspoons minced garlic
2 teaspoons minced ginger
    root
⅓ cup soy sauce

3 tablespoons dry sherry
½ teaspoon ground black
    pepper
2 tablespoons chopped
    scallions
½ cup toasted sesame
    seeds
2 tablespoons peanut or
    vegetable oil

Wash and dry the chicken wings. Snip off the wing tips, then cut wings between the wing bones and second joint.

In a bowl, mix all remaining ingredients except the sesame seeds and oil. Add chicken wings and let marinate 2 hours. Drain and roll each wing in the sesame seeds.

Brush a 20-inch piece of heavy-duty aluminum foil with oil. Prick in several places. Place foil on a large rack, 4 inches over the heat. Arrange the wings in a single layer. Grill 10 minutes, turn wings over, and grill 10 minutes longer. Serve as an appetizer or main course.

Serves 12 as an appetizer, 6 as main course.

Chinese Honey Duck

1 4–5 pound duck, split	3 tablespoons dry sherry
2 teaspoons salt	¼ cup honey
2 cloves garlic, minced	1 cup boiling water
3 tablespoons soy sauce	

Wash, clean, and dry the duck halves. Remove as much fat as possible. Mix salt, garlic, soy sauce, sherry, and honey. Rub mixture into the duck and let stand until dry. Then rub duck again with the mixture. Mix leftover honey mixture with the boiling water.

Put duck on a greased double-hinged wire grill and place about 6 inches over the heat, placing drip pan underneath. Grill 1¼ hours, basting frequently with the honey mixture and turning duck several times.

Serves 4.

Broiled Duck, Danish Style

1 5-pound duck, quartered
½ cup apple juice
¼ cup wine vinegar
3½ teaspoons salt
½ teaspoon freshly ground
    black pepper

2 bay leaves, crumbled
2 apples
2 tablespoons sugar
8 cooked or canned
    prunes

Wash and dry the duck. Cut away as much fat as possible.

In a glass or pottery bowl, or in a glass baking pan, mix apple juice, vinegar, 2 teaspoons salt, pepper, and bay leaves. Marinate duck in mixture 3 hours, basting and turning frequently. Drain, reserving marinade.

Arrange the duck quarters on greased grill 6 inches over heat, skin side up. Sprinkle with half the remaining salt. Place a drip pan underneath. Grill 25 minutes, basting several times. Turn over, skin side down. Sprinkle with remaining salt and grill an additional 25 minutes.

Wash, quarter, and core the apples while the duck is cooking. Cut two pieces of aluminum foil, each about 6 inches long. Put an apple on each, and sprinkle with sugar. Fold up foil, sealing the edges carefully. Place on grill, and cook 30 minutes, turning the packets several times.

Arrange the duck on a platter with the apples and prunes around it.

Serves 4.

Spiced Duck, Thai Style

1 5-pound duck
2 cups soy sauce
1 cup sliced onion
4 cloves garlic

2 cloves
¼ teaspoon dried red
    pepper flakes
2 anise seeds

Clean, wash, and dry the duck. Combine in a deep saucepan with soy sauce, onion, garlic, and spices. Add water to cover and cook over medium heat for 1 hour. Drain thoroughly, dry, and chill duck.

Spit the duck securely with drip pan underneath. Roast for 1 hour. The duck may be quartered or cut into small pieces through the bone when done.

Serves 4–8.

Stuffed Duck on a Spit, Indian Style

1 5-pound duck	½ cup grated onion
2 teaspoons salt	3 tablespoons butter
¾ teaspoon freshly ground black pepper	1 pound dried figs, coarsely chopped
1 teaspoon crushed anise seeds	1 teaspoon cinnamon
	1 cup unflavored yogurt
2 teaspoons crushed coriander seeds	1 cup ground blanched almonds

Wash the duck and remove as much fat as possible. Put duck in boiling water for 5 minutes. Drain and dry thoroughly.

Mix salt, pepper, anise, coriander, and onion, then rub the duck inside and out. Let stand 1 hour.

Melt butter in a skillet, add figs and cinnamon. Cook, stirring steadily, for 2 minutes. Cool, then stuff the duck. Close the opening of the duck with small skewers, then truss.

Spit the duck securely with drip pan underneath. Cook 45 minutes, then baste every few minutes with a mixture of the yogurt and almonds for an additional hour.

Serves 4.

Partridges with Grapes, German Style

4 partridges or Rock Cornish hens	8 juniper berries, coarsely crushed
2 teaspoons salt	8 slices bacon
¾ teaspoon freshly ground black pepper	½ cup dry red wine
2 cups seedless grapes	½ cup chicken broth
	½ cup sour cream

Wash and dry the birds. Coarsely chop livers and gizzards. Season the birds with salt and pepper. Combine grapes, juniper berries, and chopped livers and gizzards and divide into cavities. Wrap 2 slices of bacon around each bird and truss the birds.

Put birds in a greased double-hinged wire grill, placed 5 inches over heat with drip pan underneath. Grill 25 minutes, turning and basting frequently with wine. Remove the bacon and discard. Continue roasting birds 25 minutes, then transfer them to a heated platter and cover with foil to keep warm.

Pour the drippings into a saucepan and skim the fat. Add broth; bring to a boil and, over low heat, very gradually stir in sour cream. Do not let boil after the sour cream is added.

If desired, garnish birds with bunches of grapes, and serve the sauce in a sauceboat.

Serves 4.

Rock Cornish Hens, Japanese Style

8 Rock Cornish hens	1½ cups chicken broth
3 teaspoons salt	2 cloves garlic, sliced
1 teaspoon freshly ground black pepper	2 teaspoons ground ginger
	1 onion, sliced
1 cup soy sauce	1 cup apricot jam

Thaw, if hens are frozen. Wash and dry them. Rub, inside and out, with salt and pepper. Place in a large bowl.

In a blender container, combine soy sauce, broth, garlic, ginger, onion, and jam. Blend until smooth. Pour over hens. Marinate overnight in the refrigerator, basting several times.

Drain hens, reserving marinade. Arrange the hens on a greased rack 6 inches above heat with drip pan underneath. Grill 1 hour, turning hens every 10 minutes and brushing with marinade. Lower the rack to 4 inches above heat and grill 15 minutes longer, turning to brown all sides.

Serves 8.

Glazed Squab, Japanese Style

4 squabs, cut in half	2 cloves garlic, minced
1½ teaspoons salt	1 cup sweet sherry
½ teaspoon freshly ground black pepper	¼ cup soy sauce
	4 tablespoons sugar

Wash and dry the squabs. Rub with mixture of salt, pepper, and garlic, then put squabs in a bowl.

Bring the sherry, soy sauce, and sugar to a boil. Cool, then pour over squabs. Let marinate 4 hours at room temperature, or overnight in the refrigerator.

When ready to cook, drain, reserving the marinade. Arrange squabs on a greased double-hinged wire grill with drip pan underneath. Grill 5 inches over heat for 20 minutes on each side, brushing frequently with marinade.

Serves 4–8.

Grilled Squab, Italian Style

6 squabs	2 cloves garlic, minced
2 teaspoons salt	¾ cup lemon juice
¾ teaspoon freshly ground black pepper	¾ cup olive oil
	½ teaspoon oregano

Split the squabs down the back. Flatten slightly with a cleaver. Clean, wash, and dry. Rub squabs with mixture of salt, pepper, and garlic. Mix the remaining ingredients. Marinate squabs in the mixture for 2 hours. Drain, reserving marinade.

Arrange the squabs on a greased double-hinged wire grill with drip pan beneath. Broil 4 inches over heat for 45 minutes, basting frequently with marinade and turning grill to cook both sides.

Serves 6–12.

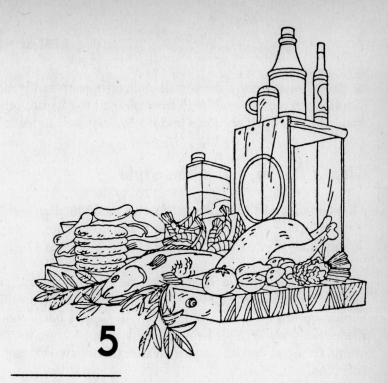

5

Meat

AN OUTDOOR BARBECUE, to the vast majority of people, usually means grilling steaks, hamburgers, or frankfurters, or—on occasion—chicken. But there is a whole world of meat barbecuing, and people who limit themselves to familiar items are missing a great deal. Many of the recipes that follow use less-expensive cuts of meat, many of them made tender by the use of marinades (which flavor the meat at the same time). Most Americans seem to prefer and use beef, but there are also recipes using pork, lamb, and veal, all of which can be prepared superbly on a grill. Surprise your family and friends with recipes collected from all over the world; other countries also cook outdoors and do so very well indeed.

Glazed Bacon, Canadian Style

1 3-pound piece Canadian bacon	½ cup medium sherry
½ cup honey	½ teaspoon nutmeg
	12 cloves

Coat bacon with a mixture of the honey, sherry, and nutmeg. Stud with the cloves. Put a large piece of heavy-duty aluminum foil on a rack and prick foil. Center bacon on it. Place rack 4 inches over heat and cook bacon 1 hour, turning often. To serve, carve into ¼-inch slices. Serve with peaches and peas.

Serves 6–8.

Barbecued Beef, Southern Style

1 5-pound fillet of beef	2 tablespoons cider vinegar
¼ pound (1 stick) butter	2 tablespoons olive oil
2 tablespoons dry red wine	¼ cup ketchup
2 teaspoons salt	½ teaspoon Tabasco
2 tablespoons Worcestershire sauce	2 tablespoons lemon juice
	3 cloves garlic, minced

Rinse and dry the meat. Combine all remaining ingredients in saucepan. Bring to a boil, stirring until butter melts. Pour mixture over meat and let stand 1 hour, basting frequently. Drain meat, reserving marinade in a saucepan.

Place meat on a greased rack 3 inches over heat. Brown 5 minutes on each side. Raise rack to 4 inches over heat and cook an additional 20 minutes, turning once. Reheat marinade and serve as a sauce.

Serves 8–10.

Barbecued Beef Ribs, Korean Style

6 pounds short ribs of beef
½ cup sugar
1 cup soy sauce
2 tablespoons minced ginger
1 tablespoon minced garlic
1 cup minced scallions
¼ cup ground sesame seeds
1 tablespoon freshly ground black pepper
¼ cup sesame-seed oil

Cut the ribs into 2-inch lengths. Toss ribs with sugar and mix all remaining ingredients. Marinate the meat in the mixture for 1 hour. Drain, reserving marinade.

Arrange the ribs on a greased double-hinged wire grill. Place 6 inches over heat. Grill 1 hour, turning and basting with the marinade several times.

Serves 8–10.

Beef Barbecue, Korean Style

2 flank steaks (about 4 pounds)
½ cup soy sauce
½ cup finely chopped scallions
6 cloves garlic, minced
4 tablespoons Chinese sesame-seed oil
4 tablespoons sesame seeds
¼ cup sugar
3 tablespoons dry sherry
¾ teaspoons freshly ground black pepper

If you're going to use a large outdoor grill, leave the 2 steaks in one piece, but score them in a crisscross pattern. If you're using a hibachi, cut the steaks across the grain in thin slices. Score each slice with an X.

Combine all remaining ingredients in a bowl, marinating meat 4 hours. Baste and turn frequently to coat all sides. Drain the meat. Grill the whole steaks 4 inches over heat for 5 minutes on each side, brushing several times with marinade. Or you may grill the slices close to heat for 2 minutes on each side.

Serves 6–8.

French Stuffed Beef Rolls

12 slices fillet of beef, ¼ inch thick
¾ cup dry red wine
1 clove garlic, minced
¼ teaspoon thyme, crumbled
1½ teaspoons salt
½ teaspoon freshly ground black pepper

2 tablespoons butter
6 chicken livers, cut in halves
½ cup minced shallots, or white part of green onions (scallions)

Flatten the beef by pounding it lightly. Mix wine, garlic, thyme, 1 teaspoon of salt, and ¼ teaspoon pepper. Marinate beef in mixture for 3 hours at room temperature.

Melt butter in a skillet; then add the livers and cook over high heat 2 minutes, turning to brown all sides. Sprinkle with remaining salt and pepper. Sprinkle each piece of steak with some of the shallots and place a half liver on each. Roll up meat and fasten with metal skewers (or tie with thread).

Arrange the rolls on a greased double-hinged wire grill. Place 4 inches over heat and grill 15 minutes. Baste with marinade and turn several times.
Serves 6.

Fillet of Beef, Taiwan Style

1 4-pound fillet of beef
1 cup soy sauce
½ cup dry sherry
2 tablespoons grated
    ginger

1 teaspoon Chinese five-
    spice powder

Tie the fillet securely. Mix all remaining ingredients. Marinate meat in mixture in the refrigerator for 24 hours, turning meat several times. Drain when ready to cook, reserving marinade.
Put the fillet on a grill, 5 inches over heat. Grill for 40 minutes, basting and turning frequently. Carve thin slices.
Serves 8–10.

Beef Rib Steak, Rumanian Style

2 ribs of beef, each cut 2
    inches thick
3 cloves garlic, minced
½ cup lemon juice

Salt
Freshly ground black
    pepper

Rinse and dry the meat. Mix the garlic into the lemon juice with a fork. Brush both sides of meat with mixture. Let stand at room temperature for 2 hours.
Arrange on a grill 5 inches over heat. Grill 10 minutes on

each side. Sprinkle with salt and pepper and slice across the grain.

Serves 4–6.

Glazed Franks, California Style

12 beef frankfurters	2 tablespoons molasses
1 cup pineapple juice	2 cloves garlic, minced
½ cup chili sauce	½ teaspoon dry mustard
2 tablespoons cider vinegar	12 toasted frankfurter rolls

Separate the franks, rinse, and dry.

Combine all remaining ingredients except the rolls in a saucepan. Bring to a boil, and cook over low heat for 10 minutes. Cool. Dip each frank into sauce, then arrange on a grill 5 inches over heat. Grill 10 minutes, turning several times, to brown on all sides. While franks are grilling, reheat sauce.

Serve franks in the rolls, with hot sauce spooned over.

Serves 12.

Glazed Ham Steaks, Costa Rican Style

2 center cut ham steaks (about 1½ pounds each)	2 tablespoons honey
	¼ cup dry sherry
	¼ cup red wine vinegar
2 tablespoons prepared mustard	¼ cup ketchup

Make small cuts around the fat of the ham steaks to prevent curling. Mix all remaining ingredients and brush both sides of the steaks with some of the mixture.

Place on a greased double-hinged wire grill. Place 6 inches above heat. Grill 20 minutes, turning and brushing with sauce several times.
Serves 6–8.

Grilled Ham, Costa Rican Style

1 4-pound canned Polish ham
1 cup chili sauce
½ cup dry sherry
½ cup brown sugar

Score the ham lightly. Cut a large piece of heavy-duty aluminum foil and prick several times. Place ham on top and put rack 4 inches over heat. Cook 1 hour, brushing frequently with a mixture of chili sauce, sherry, and brown sugar. Turn ham several times to cook evenly. Serve in thin slices.
Serves 8–10.

Ham Steak, Taiwan Style

2 2-pound ham steaks, 1½ inches thick
¼ cup cider vinegar
¼ cup dry sherry
2 tablespoons soy sauce
¼ cup honey
2 cloves garlic, minced
1 teaspoon dry mustard

Marinate ham steaks in mixture of all remaining ingredients for 3 hours at room temperature or overnight in the refrigerator. Turn steaks frequently.
When ready to grill, drain, reserving marinade. Put the steaks in a greased double-hinged wire grill and place 5 inches over heat. Grill 30 minutes, basting and turning several times.
Serves 8–10.

Barbecued Lamb Shanks, Argentine Style

6 lamb shanks	¼ cup chopped parsley
1 tablespoon salt	3 cloves garlic
1 teaspoon freshly ground	⅛ teaspoon marjoram
black pepper	¼ teaspoon dry mustard
½ cup chopped onion	⅛ teaspoon Tabasco
1 green pepper, sliced	1 cup medium sherry
2 tomatoes, diced	½ cup vegetable oil

Rinse and dry the lamb shanks. Rub with salt and pepper. Put in a bowl. Combine all remaining ingredients in a blender container. Blend for a few seconds, then pour over shanks. Cover and let marinate overnight in the refrigerator. Turn shanks several times.

When ready to cook, drain shanks, reserving marinade. Arrange on a rack 6 inches above heat with a drip pan underneath. Grill 1¼ hours, basting frequently with marinade, turning several times, to brown all sides. Heat remaining marinade and serve as a sauce.

Serves 6.

Barbecued Lamb Steaks, Australian Style

6 lamb steaks, ¾ inch	2 cloves garlic, minced
thick	2 teaspoons salt
1 cup vegetable oil	¾ teaspoon freshly ground
1 cup dry vermouth	black pepper
1 tablespoon lemon juice	½ teaspoon basil
½ cup minced onions	

Trim fat from the lamb steaks. Combine all remaining ingredients in a glass or pottery bowl. Marinate steaks in mixture for 4 hours at room temperature, turning several times. Drain and place about 5 inches over heat. Grill 20 minutes, frequently turning the steaks and basting with the marinade.

Serves 6.

Barbecued Shoulder Chops, Anglo-Indian Style

12 shoulder lamb chops, 1 inch thick
1½ teaspoons salt
½ teaspoon freshly ground black pepper
½ cup finely chopped chutney
2 tablespoons curry powder
2 tablespoons lemon juice
1 teaspoon ginger
2 tablespoons vegetable oil

Rinse and dry the chops. Season with salt and pepper. In a small saucepan, heat all remaining ingredients for 5 minutes.

Brush lamb with the chutney mixture. Arrange on a greased grill, 5 inches over heat. Cook 7 minutes on each side (or to desired degree of doneness). Brush frequently with the chutney mixture.

Serves 6–8.

Glazed Lamb Chops, Melbourne Style

8 loin lamb chops, 1½ inches thick
2 teaspoons salt
½ teaspoon freshly ground black pepper
½ cup ground walnuts
½ cup honey

Rinse and dry the chops. Season with salt and pepper. Then mix walnuts and honey.

Arrange the chops on a grill 4 inches above heat. Grill 5 minutes on each side. Spread the walnut mixture on both sides and grill 2 minutes more on each side.

Serves 4–8.

Lamb in Apricot Sauce, African Style

3 pounds lamb steak, ½ inch thick	⅛ teaspoon cayenne pepper
2 tablespoons vegetable oil	3 tablespoons cider vinegar
2 cups chopped onions	2 tablespoons grated orange rind
1 clove garlic, minced	
1 cup apricot jam	
2 teaspoons salt	

Cut the lamb steak into 8 pieces. Place pieces in a single layer in a large dish.

Heat oil in a skillet; sauté onions 10 minutes, stirring frequently. Mix in remaining ingredients. Bring to a boil, cook 1 minute, then remove from heat. When cool, pour over lamb, turning the pieces to coat both sides. Marinate in the refrigerator overnight, turning several times.

Drain the meat when ready to cook, reserving marinade. Arrange meat on a greased double-hinged wire grill. Place 5 inches over heat and grill 5 minutes on each side. While meat is cooking, reheat marinade. Serve in a sauceboat.

Serves 8.

Lamb Chops, French Style

8 loin lamb chops, 1½
inches thick
¼ teaspoon crumbled
rosemary
½ cup dry white wine

¼ cup melted butter
Salt
Freshly ground black
pepper

Rinse and dry the chops. Mix rosemary, wine, and butter. Marinate the chops in the mixture for 2 hours, turning several times. Drain, reserving marinade.

Arrange chops on a greased grill 5 inches over heat. Grill 8 minutes on each side (or to desired degree). Baste several times. Sprinkle with salt and pepper before serving.

Serves 8.

Lamb Ribs, Indonesian Style

4 pounds breast of lamb
¼ cup lemon juice
3 tablespoons soy sauce
1 teaspoon salt
1 tablespoon minced
ginger root
¼ teaspoon dried ground
chili pepper

1 teaspoon ground
coriander seed
2 teaspoons sugar
2 cloves garlic, minced
½ cup chicken broth

Cut the lamb into sections of 3 ribs each. Rinse and dry.

In a glass or pottery bowl, mix together all remaining ingredients. Add ribs, turning to coat. Cover and let marinate in the refrigerator overnight or at room temperature for 3 hours. Baste several times.

Drain ribs, reserving marinade. Arrange ribs on a double-hinged wire grill. Place 6 inches over heat and grill 1 hour, basting and turning several times.

Serves 4–6.

Marinated Lamb, New Zealand Style

1 6-pound leg of lamb	½ teaspoon marjoram
2 teaspoons salt	1 cup chopped onions
¾ teaspoon freshly ground	½ cup olive oil
black pepper	½ cup dry red wine
½ teaspoon thyme	

Bone the lamb and split in half, to open like a book. Rub lamb with a mixture of salt, pepper, thyme, and marjoram. Place lamb flat in a pan. Mix onions, oil, and wine. Pour mixture over lamb. Let marinate overnight in the refrigerator or for at least 4 hours at room temperature.

Drain the meat, reserving the marinade. Place the lamb on a greased rack with a drip pan underneath. Grill 4 inches over heat, 20 minutes on each side, basting occasionally with marinade. Slice and serve.

Serves 8–10.

Barbecued Pork Chops, Mayan Style

6 pork chops, 1 inch thick	½ teaspoon freshly ground
1 cup water	pepper
½ cup cider vinegar	1 teaspoon minced garlic
½ cup chili sauce	2 tablespoons sugar
½ cup chopped onions	1 teaspoon Worcestershire
1½ teaspoons salt	sauce

Trim fat from pork and place chops in a glass or pottery bowl. Combine remaining ingredients and bring to a boil; cook over low heat 5 minutes. Pour over chops and marinate 1 hour. Drain the chops, reserving the marinade.

Cut a piece of heavy-duty aluminum foil large enough to hold the chops in a single layer. Place on a rack, prick in several places, and arrange the chops on it. Put rack 4 inches over heat. Grill 30 to 40 minutes on each side, until no pink shows in center, basting frequently with the marinade.

Serves 6.

Chinese Red Pork

4 pounds boneless loin of pork in 1 piece	3 tablespoons dry sherry
2 scallions, chopped	8 drops red vegetable food coloring
¼ cup finely chopped ginger root	2 teaspoons Chinese sesame-seed oil
6 tablespoons soy sauce	½ cup hot water
6 tablespoons hoisin sauce	2 tablespoons sherry

Rinse and dry the pork. Prick the surface thoroughly with a sharp fork.

Mix scallions, ginger, soy sauce, hoisin sauce, sherry, and food coloring. Rub the mixture into the pork. Place in a bowl, cover, and refrigerate overnight. Baste several times.

Put the pork on a greased double-hinged wire grill and place grill 6 inches over heat with a drip pan underneath. Cook 1¼ hours, turning the meat several times. Mix sesame-seed oil, water, and honey. Brush to coat meat and cook 10 to 15 minutes on each side, until no pink shows in center. Let cool 15 minutes before cutting thin slices. Serve with hot Chinese mustard.

Serves 8–10.

Grilled Pork Chops, Danish Style

8 rib pork chops, 1 inch thick
¾ cup dry white wine
1 tablespoon lemon juice
1½ teaspoons salt
½ teaspoon freshly ground black pepper
1 clove garlic, minced
2 bay leaves, crumbled
1 teaspoon caraway seeds

Trim fat from chops. Rinse and dry.

In a large glass bowl or baking dish, combine all remaining ingredients. Add the chops and turn several times, coating with marinade. Cover and refrigerate 4 hours or overnight, basting several times. Drain, reserving the marinade.

Arrange chops on a greased rack 5 inches over heat. Grill 30 minutes on each side, brushing with marinade, until no pink shows in center.

Serves 4–8.

Grilled Pork Chops, Lebanese

12 rib or loin pork chops, ¾ inch thick
2 teaspoons salt
¾ teaspoon freshly ground black pepper
2 teaspoons minced garlic
1½ teaspoons crumbled oregano
½ teaspoon crumbled mint
3 lemons, quartered

Rinse and dry the chops. Mix salt, pepper, garlic, oregano, and mint. Rub mixture into both sides of chops. Let stand 30 minutes.

Arrange chops on a grill 6 inches over heat. Grill 20 to 30 minutes on each side or until no pink shows in center. Serve with lemon quarters.

Serves 6–12.

Grilled Pork Cutlets, Dubrovnik Style

2 pounds boneless loin of
    pork
2 teaspoons salt
¾ teaspoon freshly ground
    black pepper

2 cups chopped onions
    Thinly sliced onions

Cut the meat into 8 equal slices.

Put in a bowl, sprinkle with salt and pepper, then cover with chopped onions. Cover and refrigerate overnight.

Remove meat and grill 5 inches over heat for 10 minutes on each side. Serve with thinly sliced onions.

Serves 4–8.

Korean Sesame Pork

3 pork tenderloins
½ cup soy sauce
¼ cup chopped green
    onions
2 cloves garlic, minced

½ teaspoon freshly ground
    black pepper
1 teaspoon ground ginger
½ cup sesame seeds

Wash and dry the pork tenderloins (if not available, have the butcher bone a 10-inch loin of pork and cut it into 3 strips). Mix all remaining ingredients, and marinate pork in the mixture for 2 hours at room temperature. Drain, but be sure the sesame seeds adhere to the pork. Place on the grill about 5 inches over heat and grill 45 to 55 minutes, until no pink shows in the center (thermometer should register 185° F.). Turn and baste frequently. Cut into thin slices.

Serves 6–8.

Roast Smoked Pork Loin, German Style

4 pounds smoked pork loin	1 cup dry white wine
4 juniper berries, coarsely crushed	1 cup chopped onions
	1 cup grated carrots

Cut the backbone of the loin every half inch to facilitate carving. It should be left attached and tied to the loin in several places, however. Rub the loin thoroughly with the crushed juniper berries.

Spit pork securely and place on grill. With drip pan underneath, pour wine, onions, and carrots on. Roast 2 hours (175° F. on a meat thermometer), basting several times with wine mixture.

Purée pan juices in a blender and reheat, skimming fat. Taste for seasoning.

Remove strings from pork and carve ½-inch-thick chops. Serve with sauce.

Serves 6–8.

Barbecued Spareribs with Beer, Manila Style

2 racks spareribs (about 4½ pounds)	1 teaspoon ground cumin seed
3 cups beer	1 teaspoon paprika
1 cup honey	1 tablespoon salt
1½ teaspoons dry mustard	2 tablespoons lemon juice

Rinse and dry the spareribs. Cut each rack into 4 pieces. Put in a glass bowl or stainless-steel pan. Combine remaining ingredients and pour over ribs. Cover and marinate in the refrigerator overnight, turning occasionally.

Drain ribs, reserving marinade. Cut a piece of heavy-duty aluminum foil large enough to hold the ribs in a single layer. Put the foil on the rack, and prick in several places. Place 5 to 6 inches over the heat. Arrange the ribs on it. Cook, turning frequently and brushing with the marinade, 1¼ hours or until browned.

Serves 4–6.

Chinese Spareribs

2 racks spareribs (about 4½ pounds)
⅓ cup soy sauce
⅓ cup honey
3 tablespoons cider vinegar
1 tablespoon sugar
1 teaspoon ground ginger
2 tablespoons dry sherry
1½ cups beef broth
2 cloves garlic, minced

Crack the spareribs through the middle. Combine all remaining ingredients in a large bowl. Marinate ribs in mixture for 3 hours at room temperature or overnight in the refrigerator. Baste and turn several times.

Drain ribs and put on a double-hinged wire grill. Place 5 to 6 inches over heat and grill 1¼ hours, basting with the marinade and turning frequently. To serve, cut into individual ribs. Pass the remaining marinade to spoon over ribs.

Serves 4–6.

Garlic Spareribs, Vietnamese Style

2 racks spareribs (about 4 pounds), cracked
12 cloves garlic
2 slices ginger root
1 teaspoon anise seed
1 teaspoon cinnamon
1 tablespoon salt
1 tablespoon sugar
¼ cup dry sherry
¾ cup soy sauce

Wash and dry the spareribs. Combine the garlic, spices, salt, sugar, and sherry in a blender container. Blend a few seconds, then mix into the soy sauce. Pour over spareribs, turning to coat both sides. Let stand 2 hours, basting several times.

Cut a piece of heavy-duty aluminum foil large enough to hold the ribs in a single layer. Place on a rack and prick with a fork in several places. Arrange spareribs on foil. Broil 4 inches over heat for 1 hour, turning the ribs once. Cut into individual ribs.

Serves 4–8.

German Spareribs

2 racks spareribs (about 4½ pounds)	1 clove garlic, minced
3 teaspoons salt	1 pound sauerkraut (fresh if available)
¾ teaspoon freshly ground black pepper	2 teaspoons caraway seeds
	Oil

Leave the racks of spareribs in one piece. Rinse and dry. Rub ribs with a mixture of salt, pepper, and garlic. Place in a bowl and add sauerkraut and caraway seeds. Marinate in the refrigerator overnight, or 2 hours at room temperature.

Cut 2 pieces of heavy-duty aluminum foil long enough for each rack of ribs. Prick in several places, then brush with oil. Place on a rack 4 inches above heat. Arrange drained ribs on foil. Grill 30 minutes on each side. Remove top foil. Spread the top half of the ribs with the sauerkraut. Grill 10 minutes. Turn over (some of the sauerkraut will fall off), and spread the remaining sauerkraut on top. Grill 10 minutes. To serve, cut ribs into sections.

Serves 4–6.

Spareribs, California Style

2 racks spareribs (about
    4½ pounds)
1½ cups ketchup
2 tablespoons dry mustard
2 tablespoons vegetable
    oil
½ teaspoon Tabasco
2 tablespoons
    Worcestershire sauce
2 teaspoons salt
¾ teaspoon freshly ground
    black pepper

Cut the ribs into 2 sections. Mix remaining ingredients in a bowl. Coat ribs with mixture and let stand 2 hours, turning several times.

Arrange ribs on a grill 6 inches over heat, and grill 1¼ hours, turning and basting frequently.

Serves 4–6.

Spareribs, Hawaiian Style

2 racks spareribs (about
    4½ pounds)
1½ teaspoons salt
2 cups pineapple juice
⅓ cup soy sauce
⅓ cup honey
⅓ cup ketchup
2 tablespoons dry sherry
2 cloves garlic, minced
2 teaspoons minced
    ginger root

Start the preparation a day in advance.

Cut the ribs into 2 sections. Rinse and dry. Combine in a saucepan with the salt and pineapple juice. Bring to a boil, cover, and cook over low heat 45 minutes. Drain, reserving ½ cup of the liquid.

Arrange ribs in a single layer in a glass or stainless-steel baking pan. Mix together remaining ingredients and reserved liquid. Pour over ribs and turn several times to coat both sides. Cover and marinate in the refrigerator overnight, turning several times.

When ready to cook, drain the ribs, reserving the marinade. Arrange ribs on a greased double-hinged wire grill. Place 5 inches over heat and grill 25 minutes, turning and basting with marinade several times.

Serves 4–6.

Spareribs with Pickle Sauce, Swedish Style

2 racks spareribs (about 4½ pounds)
2 teaspoons salt
¾ teaspoon freshly ground black pepper
1 bay leaf, crumbled
2 cups beer
2 tablespoons vegetable oil
1 cup minced onions
⅛ teaspoon powdered allspice
1 clove, crushed
1 tablespoon flour
2 tablespoons tomato paste
1 cup chopped dill pickle

Cut the spareribs into 2 sections. Rinse and dry. Mix salt, pepper, bay leaf, and beer. Marinate ribs in mixture for 1 hour, basting several times. Drain, reserving marinade.

Arrange ribs on a greased double-hinged wire grill. Place 5 to 6 inches over heat and grill 1¼ hours, turning several times. While the ribs are grilling, prepare the sauce.

Heat the oil in a skillet. Sauté onions 5 minutes. Blend in allspice, cloves, flour, and tomato paste. Add marinade, stirring constantly. Bring to a boil, stirring steadily, then cook over low heat for 10 minutes. Serve in a sauceboat to spoon over ribs.

Serves 4–6.

Texas Spareribs

2 racks spareribs (about
   4½ pounds)
1 cup cider vinegar
1 cup water
3 tablespoons butter
2 tablespoons
   Worcestershire sauce

½ teaspoon Tabasco
½ teaspoon dry mustard
2 teaspoons sugar
1 teaspoon chili powder
2 cloves garlic, minced
1 cup minced onions
½ cup chili sauce

Crack the ribs through the middle and place in a bowl. Combine all remaining ingredients in a saucepan and bring to a boil. Pour over spareribs, and let marinate at room temperature for 3 hours. Drain, reserving marinade.

Put ribs on a greased double-hinged wire grill. Place 5 to 6 inches over heat and grill 1¼ hours, basting and turning frequently. Heat remaining marinade over low heat for 20 minutes; serve as a sauce. Cut spareribs into individual ribs. Serves 4–6.

Barbecued Flank Steak

2 2-pound flank steaks
½ cup olive or vegetable
   oil
4 tablespoons wine
   vinegar

1½ teaspoons salt
⅛ teaspoon hot red-pepper
   sauce
½ teaspoon thyme
1 clove garlic, minced

Marinate steaks in the mixture of all ingredients for 2 hours at room temperature. Drain, reserving the marinade.

Place meat about 5 inches above the heat and broil 4 minutes on each side, basting several times with marinade. Carve in thin diagonal slices. Serves 6–8.

Grilled Flank Steak, Bulgarian Style

1 flank steak (about 1½ pounds)
¼ cup red wine vinegar
1 tablespoon tomato paste
2 cloves garlic, minced
1 cup hot water
1½ teaspoons salt
½ teaspoon freshly ground black pepper
1 bay leaf, crumbled
½ teaspoon oregano
2 tablespoons vegetable oil

Score the steak in a crisscross pattern.

In an oblong glass or pottery pan, mix together all remaining ingredients. Add meat and turn several times to coat with the marinade. Cover and let stand in the refrigerator overnight or for at least 3 hours at room temperature, basting several times. Drain, reserving marinade.

Place the meat on a greased rack 4 inches over heat, and grill 5 minutes on each side, basting with marinade. To serve, cut into thin slices diagonally across the grain.

Serves 2–4.

Mexican Flank Steak

1 flank steak
¼ cup olive oil
2 tablespoons wine vinegar
1½ teaspoons salt
⅛ teaspoon Tabasco
1 teaspoon oregano, crushed
1 teaspoon chili powder
1 clove garlic, minced

Marinate the steak in a mixture of all remaining ingredients for 2 hours at room temperature. Drain, reserving the marinade. Place steak on a greased rack 5 inches over the

heat and grill 4 minutes on each side, basting several times with marinade. Carve in thin diagonal slices.
Serves 4.

Breaded Steak, Italian Style

2 2-inch-thick T-bone
    steaks
1 cup olive oil
2 cloves garlic, minced
¾ cup dry breadcrumbs

½ cup grated Parmesan
    cheese
½ teaspoon freshly ground
    black pepper
½ teaspoon oregano

Trim fat from steaks. Mix oil and garlic, then dip both sides of the steaks in it. Let stand 1 hour, basting frequently. Drain.

Mix breadcrumbs, cheese, pepper, and oregano. Dip the steaks in the mixture, coating both sides. Arrange on an oiled double-hinged wire grill. Grill 4 inches over heat, 10 minutes on each side, or to desired degree of rareness. Slice and serve.
Serves 6–8.

Broiled Steak, Japanese Style

1½ pounds sirloin steak, ¾
    inch thick
½ cup soy sauce
¼ cup sake or sherry
2 tablespoons sugar

1 clove garlic, minced
2 tablespoons minced
    ginger root
Chopped green onions
    (optional)

Pound meat with a cleaver or knife to ½-inch thickness. Mix soy sauce, sake (a Japanese liquor) or sherry, sugar, garlic, and ginger. Marinate the steak 4 hours at room temperature or overnight in the refrigerator. Drain and place on a greased double-hinged wire grill. Broil 2 minutes on each side, 4 inches over heat, or to desired degree of rareness. Serve with chopped green onions, if desired.

Serves 4.

Broiled Steak, Roquefort Style

4 2-inch-thick club (shell) steaks	1 teaspoon Worcestershire sauce
½ stick (⅛ pound) unsalted butter	2 tablespoons minced chives or scallions
½ pound Roquefort cheese	

Rinse, dry, and trim fat from steak. Cream butter with cheese, Worcestershire sauce, and chives or scallions.

Arrange steaks on a greased grill, 5 inches above heat. Grill 10 minutes. Turn and spread each steak with cheese mixture. Grill an additional 10 minutes longer, or to desired degree of rareness. Slice or cut in half to serve.

Serves 6–8.

Carpet-Bag Steak (Australia)

3 pounds fillet of beef	1½ teaspoons salt
12 shucked oysters	½ teaspoon freshly ground black pepper
½ cup thinly sliced mushrooms	Olive oil

Slit fillet lengthwise (so that it opens like a book). Arrange the oysters on the fillet and cover with mushrooms. Then close the steak, securing the edges with metal skewers or thread.

Season fillet with salt and pepper and brush with olive oil. Grill 4 inches above heat 5 minutes on each side. Then raise grill to 6 inches above heat and cook 5 minutes longer on each side (or to desired degree of rareness). To serve, carve into 2-inch-thick slices.

Serves 6–8.

Grilled Steak, Venezuelan Style

6 chuck or round steaks,
   1½ inches thick
1 teaspoon meat tenderizer
½ teaspoon oregano
1 teaspoon salt
1 teaspoon ground cumin
   seeds

⅛ teaspoon dried ground
   red peppers
2 teaspoons minced garlic
½ cup dry red wine
⅓ cup vegetable oil

Pound steaks lightly, then prick surface with a fork. Place in a single layer in a glass baking dish.

Mix all remaining ingredients. Pour over meat, turning the steaks several times to coat both sides. Marinate at room temperature for 1 hour. Turn the steaks several times. Drain, reserving the marinade.

Arrange steaks on a greased grill 5 inches over heat. Grill 20 minutes, turning and basting several times.

Serves 6.

Marinated Steak, Australian Style

3 pounds sirloin steak, 1½ inches thick
¼ cup olive oil or vegetable oil
2 tablespoons lemon juice
1 teaspoon salt
½ teaspoon freshly ground black pepper
1 clove garlic, minced
1 tablespoon minced parsley
2 tablespoons butter

Trim off all fat from steak. Mix oil, lemon juice, salt, pepper, garlic, and parsley. Marinate the steak in the mixture for 3 hours, turning and basting frequently. Drain. Grill to desired degree of rareness and place a pat of butter on each serving.
Serves 6–8.

Steak, Bolivian Style

2 shell steaks, 2 inches thick
½ cup olive oil
½ cup rum
2 cloves garlic, minced
1 teaspoon oregano
1 tablespoon chili powder
⅛ teaspoon dried ground red pepper
Salt

Trim fat from steaks. Mix all remaining ingredients except salt. Add the steaks and turn to coat all sides. Let stand in the refrigerator 4 hours, turning several times. When ready to grill, drain the steaks, reserving the marinade.

Arrange steaks on a grill 5 inches over heat. Grill 8 minutes on each side (or to desired degree of rareness), basting several times with marinade. Sprinkle with salt and serve.
Serves 2–4.

Steak with Green Peppercorns, French Style

2 shell steaks, 2 inches thick	Salt
	¼ cup cognac
3 tablespoons green peppercorns	

Trim fat from steak. Crush the peppercorns coarsely, and with the heel of the hand press them into both sides of the steak. Let stand 2 hours.

Arrange steaks on grill 5 inches over heat. Grill 8 minutes on each side (or to desired degree of rareness). Transfer to heated platter. Salt lightly. Set the cognac aflame and pour over the steaks. When flames die, carve and serve.

Serves 2–4.

Steak, Mexican Style

1 3-inch-thick sirloin steak	2 tablespoons chili powder
½ cup rum	½ teaspoon oregano
½ cup olive oil	⅛ teaspoon Tabasco
2 cloves garlic, minced	Salt

Trim fat from steak. Mix rum, oil, garlic, chili powder, oregano, and Tabasco. Marinate steak in mixture overnight in the refrigerator. Turn several times.

Drain when ready to cook. Put on a greased grill, 5 inches above heat. Grill 10 minutes on each side (or to desired degree of rareness). Sprinkle with salt and carve.

Serves 4–6.

Steak, Moroccan Style

4 pounds chuck steak, cut
   2 inches thick
Meat tenderizer
2 cups minced parsley
2 cups minced onions

2 teaspoons salt
¾ teaspoon freshly ground
   black pepper
¼ cup vegetable oil

Sprinkle the meat with tenderizer as package directs. Mix together parsley, onions, salt, and pepper. Coat meat with mixture and let stand 2 hours. Press the parsley mixture into the meat.

Put meat on a double--hinged wire grill. Sprinkle both sides with oil. Grill about 4 inches above heat, 15 minutes on each side. Serve in thin slices.

Serves 8–10.

Tartare Steak, Russian Style

6 club steaks, cut 1 inch
   thick
1¼ pounds ground beef
1½ teaspoons salt
½ teaspoon freshly ground
   black pepper

¼ cup minced scallions
   (green onions)
¼ cup minced parsley
1 tablespoon prepared
   French-style mustard

Cut the steak through the middle, leaving sides attached to open like a book. Mix all remaining ingredients and spread some on each steak. Pressing down firmly, close sides and secure with small skewers.

Arrange steaks on a greased double-hinged wire grill. Place 4 inches over heat and grill 5 minutes on each side. Serve with a cube of parsley butter on top.

Serves 6.

Grilled Mixed Meats, Mexican Style

6 chorizos (Spanish
   sausages)
2 pounds fillet of beef

1 pork tenderloin (fillet)
  Coarse (Kosher) salt

A small hibachi or Mexican clay brasero may be used for cooking meats at the table. Each person can then prepare his own. If you wish, however, you may still use a regular grill.

Cover the sausages with water, bring to a boil, and cook 20 minutes. Drain and cool. Slice beef and pork each ¼ inch thick. Place on separate plates, or arrange on a large platter.

Start cooking the pork first, placing it 2 inches above heat. Grill 15 minutes, turning to cook both sides until pink color is gone. Arrange the beef and chorizos on grill after pork has cooked 8 minutes. Turn beef and sausage to brown all sides. Sprinkle beef and pork with salt before serving. Serve with sautéed green peppers and fried bananas.

Serves 6–8.

Hungarian Chuck Roast

4 pounds chuck roast
  Meat tenderizer
3 tablespoons butter
1 cup minced onions
1 cup minced green
   pepper

1 teaspoon salt
1 tablespoon paprika
1 10½-ounce can beef
   gravy
1 cup sour cream

Tenderize meat as package directs.

Melt butter in saucepan. Add onions and green pepper; sauté 10 minutes, stirring frequently. Mix in salt and paprika, then gravy. Heat, stirring until smooth. Blend in sour cream and remove from heat.

Spread meat with some of the sauce and place on the grill about 4 inches over heat. Grill 20 minutes on each side (or until tender). Cut very thin slices.
Serves 8–10.

Saddle of Venison, Norwegian Style

3 cups dry red wine	1 5-pound saddle of
3 cups water	venison
1 cup chopped onions	6 slices bacon
1 tablespoon salt	½ cup heavy cream
8 peppercorns, crushed	Loganberries or
6 juniper berries, crushed	cranberries
2 cloves, crushed	

Combine wine, water, onions, salt, peppercorns, juniper berries, and cloves in a saucepan. Bring to a boil, cook 2 minutes, and remove from heat. Cool.

Put venison in an enamel, glass, or pottery pan or bowl. Pour marinade over venison, basting several times to moisten thoroughly. Cover and marinate in the refrigerator 48 hours, turning meat several times. (If necessary, the meat can be kept at room temperature for 6 hours, although the flavor will not be as pronounced.)

When ready to cook, drain the venison, reserving the marinade, then dry. Cut the bacon crosswise, then into ⅛-inch strips. With a larding needle, force the strips through the meat about every 2 inches.

Spit the venison securely. Pour half the marinade into a drip pan and place underneath. Roast, covered, 1 hour, basting frequently. Uncover and roast an additional hour, basting frequently. (If grill doesn't have a cover, increase roasting time 1 hour.)

Transfer venison to a heated platter. Pour drippings through a strainer into a saucepan, pressing the vegetables through. Skim the fat. Bring to a boil and gradually stir in cream. Cook over low heat for 5 more minutes. Serve in a sauceboat.

Serve with cranberries or loganberries.

Serves 6–8.

Barbecued Veal Chops, Uruguayan Style

6 veal chops, 1½ inches thick
½ cup dry red wine
¼ cup vegetable oil
¼ cup tomato sauce
½ cup minced onions
1 clove garlic, minced
1½ teaspoons salt
½ teaspoon thyme, crushed
½ teaspoon ground cumin seeds
½ teaspoon paprika
¼ teaspoon dried red pepper flakes

Rinse and dry the chops. Combine all remaining ingredients in a bowl. Marinate chops in mixture for at least 2 hours at room temperature, or overnight in the refrigerator. Turn the chops several times.

Drain the chops and arrange on a greased grill. Grill 6 inches over heat for 20 minutes on each side, brushing chops with marinade several times.

Serves 6.

Barbecued Veal Chops, Mexican Style

6 veal chops, 1½ inches
  thick
½ cup cider vinegar
¼ cup vegetable oil
¼ cup ketchup
½ teaspoon crumbled
  thyme leaves
½ teaspoon ground cumin
  seeds

½ teaspoon chili powder
¼ teaspoon ground dry red
  pepper
1½ teaspoons salt
½ cup minced onion
1 clove garlic, minced

Rinse and dry the chops.

Combine remaining ingredients in a bowl. Marinate chops in mixture 3 hours at room temperature.

Drain chops and arrange on a foil-covered rack. Grill 5 inches above heat for 15 to 20 minutes on each side or until browned and tender, basting frequently with marinade.

Serves 6.

6

Ground Meat

ASK ANY TEENAGER to name his or her favorite food, and the answer will overwhelmingly be hamburgers. A properly prepared hamburger is delicious, no doubt about it, and it's something particularly satisfying when you're hungry for a simple but tasty dish. But then, all ground meats are surprisingly versatile, and combinations of beef and veal, beef and lamb, or beef and pork offer a complete new set of interesting barbecue preparations.

Many experts think the addition of a tablespoon of ice

water to a hamburger-size patty of meat makes the finished product even more juicy and delicious. I tend to agree. However, most of these recipes have other ingredients that help to provide the proper texture and juiciness.

Ground Beef, Swiss Style

1½ pounds ground beef	2 tablespoons ice water
1½ teaspoons salt	6 slices Swiss cheese, ⅛
¼ teaspoon freshly ground	inch thick
black pepper	6 slices boiled ham

Lightly mix the beef, salt, pepper, and water, using your hands. Shape into 12 patties. Place a slice each of cheese and ham on 6 patties, tuck in overlap if any, then cover with remaining patties. Press together gently. Grill on a greased rack 4 inches over the heat, 5 to 6 minutes on each side, or until as done as desired. If desired, serve with mushroom or tomato sauce.

Serves 6.

Skinless Beef Sausages, Rumanian Style

2 pounds fatty ground beef	¼ teaspoon thyme
4 cloves garlic, minced	2 teaspoons salt
¼ teaspoon bicarbonate of soda	¾ teaspoon freshly ground black pepper
½ teaspoon ground allspice	½ cup beef broth
¼ teaspoon ground cloves	

Be sure the meat you buy has some fat. Mix together all the ingredients with your hands in a bowl. Between wet palms, shape the mixture into sausages 1 inch round and 3 inches long. Arrange on a platter. Cover and refrigerate overnight.

Remove from refrigerator 1 hour before cooking and let stand uncovered.

Grease a double-hinged wire grill and arrange the sausages on it. Place grill 4 inches above heat; broil sausages for 15 to 20 minutes, turning several times to brown all sides. Serve hot with pickles and hot peppers.

Serves 6–8.

Smyrna Beef Sausages

½ cup white breadcrumbs
¼ cup milk
1½ pounds ground beef
1 cup finely chopped
onions
1½ teaspoons salt
½ teaspoon freshly ground
black pepper

2 teaspoons chopped fresh
mint or ½ teaspoon
dried mint
3 tablespoons minced
parsley
2 eggs, beaten

Soak breadcrumbs in milk and squeeze out any liquid. Mix thoroughly with remaining ingredients. Form mixture into 2-inch sausage shapes.

Arrange the sausages on a greased double-hinged wire grill. Grill 4 inches above heat for 10 to 15 minutes, turning grill several times to brown all sides. If desired, serve with a spicy tomato sauce.

Serves 4–6.

Yugoslavian Beef Sausages

1½ pounds ground beef
¾ pound ground pork
2 teaspoons salt
½ teaspoon freshly ground
    black pepper

1 teaspoon paprika
½ cup cold water
¼ cup vegetable oil
Sliced onions

Mix beef, pork, salt, pepper, and paprika. Work in water with the hands until the mixture holds together. Form 8 sausage shapes. Brush thoroughly with oil. Place on a greased double-hinged wire grill. Broil about 6 inches above heat, 10 minutes on each side. Serve with sliced onions.
Serves 8.

Brazilian Hamburgers

2 pounds ground beef
½ cup grated Parmesan
    cheese
1 cup finely chopped
    green onions
1 cup finely chopped
    parsley

2 eggs, beaten
2 tablespoons water
1½ teaspoons salt
Dash cayenne pepper

Mix all ingredients thoroughly with hands. Form into 8 patties.
Arrange on a greased double-hinged wire grill and place about 5 inches over the fire. Grill 10 to 15 minutes, until done to preference, turning to brown both sides.
Serves 8.

Bacon-Wrapped Hamburgers, Alaskan Style

2 pounds ground beef
2 teaspoons salt
¾ teaspoon freshly ground
    black pepper

⅛ teaspoon ground allspice
16 slices bacon
Toasted hamburger buns
    or English muffins

Lightly mix beef, salt, pepper, and allspice. Shape into 8 patties. Wrap 2 slices of bacon around each. Arrange on a greased double-hinged wire grill. Grill about 5 inches over heat for 7 to 8 minutes on each side. Serve on buns or muffins. Serves 8.

Hamburgers, Israeli Style

2 pounds ground beef
2 teaspoons salt
½ teaspoon freshly ground
    black pepper
2 eggs, lightly beaten
1 cup fresh breadcrumbs
3 tablespoons minced
    parsley

1 teaspoon ground cumin
    seed
8 small pita breads
Chopped onions
Diced tomatoes
Unflavored yogurt

Mix together beef, salt, pepper, eggs, breadcrumbs, parsley, and cumin. Shape into 8 patties. Arrange on a greased double-hinged wire grill. Place 4 inches above heat and grill 5 minutes on each side.

While meat is cooking, slit the pita bread, leaving it connected. Wrap in aluminum foil and place on grill to heat. When meat is cooked, put a hamburger in each pita and spoon in some onions, tomatoes, and yogurt.

Serves 8.

Meat Loaf, Italian Style

3 tablespoons olive oil	¼ pound grated mozzarella cheese
1 cup chopped onions	
2 cloves garlic, minced	¾ cup dry breadcrumbs
2 pounds ground beef	2 teaspoons salt
1 cup chopped fresh spinach (or ½ package frozen spinach, chopped and well drained)	½ teaspoon freshly ground black pepper
	1 teaspoon crumbled oregano
	2 eggs, beaten

Heat oil in a skillet; then sauté onions and garlic 5 minutes. Place in a bowl and cool slightly. Add all remaining ingredients and mix until well blended.

Divide mixture into 8 pieces and shape each into an oblong loaf. Arrange on greased rack 6 inches over heat. Grill 20 minutes, turning several times to brown all sides. If desired, serve with the following sauce.

Serves 8.

SAUCE

1½ cups tomato sauce	½ teaspoon freshly ground black pepper
½ cup dry red wine	
½ cup minced onions	2 tablespoons olive oil
1 teaspoon salt	

Combine all ingredients in a saucepan. Bring to a boil and cook over low heat 15 minutes.
Serves 8.

South African Burgers

1½ pounds ground beef
1 pound ground fat pork
2 teaspoons salt
¾ teaspoon freshly ground
  black pepper
4 teaspoons coriander
  seeds, crushed
2 tablespoons cider
  vinegar

Mix ground beef and pork with salt, spices, and vinegar. Let stand in the refrigerator for 4 hours.

Shape mixture into 10 patties. Place on a greased double-hinged wire grill and cook about 4 inches above the heat for 20 minutes, until browned but still juicy, turning rack several times.
Serves 5–10.

Barbecued Meat Patties, Spanish Style

2 pounds ground beef
2 eggs
2 teaspoons salt
¾ teaspoon freshly ground
  black pepper
2 cloves garlic, minced
¾ cup chopped onion
½ cup finely chopped
  green pepper
⅓ cup dry breadcrumbs
1 8-ounce can Spanish style
  tomato sauce

Mix beef, eggs, salt, pepper, garlic, onions, green peppers, and breadcrumbs. Shape into 12 patties. Arrange patties on a greased double-hinged wire grill.

Grill 6 inches above heat for 15 minutes, brushing frequently with tomato sauce and turning rack several times. Heat the remaining sauce and serve with the patties.

Serves 6–8.

Ground Meat Patties, Indian Style

2 pounds ground lean beef or lamb	2 teaspoons ground cumin seeds
2 teaspoons salt	¼ teaspoon ground ginger
½ teaspoon freshly ground black pepper	¼ cup grated onion
½ teaspoon turmeric	1 clove garlic, minced
¼ teaspoon ground mustard seeds	2 tablespoons yogurt
	2 egg whites, stiffly beaten
	¼ cup melted butter

Thoroughly blend meat, salt, pepper, turmeric, mustard seeds, cumin, ginger, onion, garlic, and yogurt. Fold in beaten egg whites. Form into 8 patties.

Arrange patties on a greased double-hinged wire grill and brush with butter. Place 6 inches over heat and cook the beef for 15 minutes, lamb for 20 minutes. Turn frequently and baste often with butter.

Serves 4–8.

Meat and Lentil Patties, Indian Style

1 cup lentils
1 pound ground lamb or
    beef
1½ teaspoons salt
2 cloves garlic, minced
1 tablespoon minced
    ginger root

1 teaspoon ground
    coriander seeds
¼ teaspoon crushed mint
2 eggs, lightly beaten

Wash the lentils, cover with water, and bring to a boil. Cook over low heat for 1 hour. Drain and purée in electric blender or food processor. Cool.

Mix the lentils with all remaining ingredients. Shape into 12 patties. Arrange patties on a greased double-hinged wire grill. Grill 5 inches over the heat, 15 minutes for beef, 20 minutes for lamb. Turn several times.

Serves 6–12.

Meat Patties, Thai Style

2 pounds lean ground beef
¼ pound mushrooms, finely
    chopped
½ cup finely chopped
    scallions
¾ cup chopped water
    chestnuts

¼ cup soy sauce
2 tablespoons dry sherry
¼ teaspoon cayenne
    pepper
2 tablespoons minced
    ginger root
1 tablespoon cornstarch

Mix all ingredients until well blended. Shape into 12 patties.

Arrange on a greased double-hinged wire grill. Place 5 inches over heat and grill 7 to 8 minutes on each side. Serve with orange sauce if desired:

Combine 1 cup orange marmalade with ½ cup vinegar in a blender. Blend until smooth. Pour into small saucepan and heat.

Serves 6–12.

Mixed Meat Patties, Bucharest Style

1½ pounds ground lamb
½ pound ground beef
¼ cup minced scallions
2 tablespoons minced parsley
2 teaspoons salt

½ teaspoon thyme
1 teaspoon crushed fennel seed
⅛ teaspoon dried ground red peppers
2 egg yolks, beaten

Mix all ingredients and shape into 8 patties. Arrange on a greased double-hinged wire grill. Place 6 inches above heat and grill for 20 minutes, turning several times to brown both sides evenly.

Serves 4–8.

Mixed Meat Patties, Yugoslavian Style

1 pound ground veal
1 pound ground pork
2 teaspoons salt
1 teaspoon freshly ground black pepper

1 cup finely chopped onions

Mix all ingredients except onions together. Knead as you would a dough for several minutes. Cover and refrigerate for 3 hours. Divide the mixture into 6 large flat patties.

Place patties on a greased double-hinged wire grill. Grill on rack 5 inches above heat for 10 minutes on each side, or until no pink remains when the meat is cut in center. Serve with chopped onions and, if desired, small hot peppers.

Serves 6.

New Zealand Meat Patties

2 pounds ground beef
3 cups grated raw potato
½ cup chopped onions
2 eggs, beaten
1 cup light cream
2 teaspoons salt
½ teaspoon freshly ground black pepper

Mix beef, grated potato, onions, eggs, cream, salt, and pepper. Shape into 8 patties.

Put patties on a greased double-hinged wire grill and place about 5 inches over heat. Grill 15 to 20 minutes, turning to brown both sides.

Serves 8.

Lamb Patties, Polish Style

2 pounds ground lamb
½ pound sausage meat
1 cup peeled chopped tomatoes
1 cup minced scallions
2 teaspoons salt
¾ teaspoon freshly ground black pepper
½ teaspoon thyme
¾ cup sour cream
Olive oil

Mix together all ingredients except oil. Shape into 12 patties. Arrange on an oiled double-hinged wire grill. Brush all sides with oil. Place 6 inches above heat and grill for 20 minutes, turning and brushing with oil several times. Serve with sauerkraut and steamed potatoes if desired.

Serves 6–12.

Minced Pork Cakes, Burmese Style

1 pound ground pork	1½ teaspoons salt
½ pound raw cleaned shrimp, finely chopped	½ teaspoon freshly ground black pepper
1 cup finely chopped onions	1 teaspoon ground cumin seeds
2 cloves garlic, minced	2 eggs, beaten
1 tablespoon lime or lemon juice	

Mix all ingredients until smooth. Shape into 8 round cakes. Arrange on a greased double-hinged wire grill. Broil 5 inches above heat for 25 minutes, turning rack to brown all sides.

Serves 4–8.

Note: Smaller versions make unusual hors d'oeuvre.

Sausage Burgers, Mexican Style

2 pounds spicy bulk sausage meat (see note)	½ cup fine, dry breadcrumbs
2 eggs, beaten	2 tablespoons chili powder

Mix all ingredients. Shape into 12 round cakes and arrange on a lightly greased double-hinged grill. Grill 4 inches over heat for 20 minutes (or until no pink remains in the meat). Turn rack to brown all sides. Serve with tomato sauce, if desired.

Serves 6–12.

Note: Italian markets generally have spicy bulk sausage. If not available, buy spicy uncooked Italian sausages, and remove the casing.

Veal Patties, Armenian Style

1½ pounds ground veal
1½ cups mashed potatoes
1 egg, beaten
2½ teaspoons salt
1 teaspoon freshly ground
    black pepper

¼ cup pine nuts or
    slivered almonds,
    lightly toasted
¼ cup chopped seedless
    raisins
¼ cup melted butter

Mix all ingredients except butter in a bowl. Knead with the hands until ingredients hold together.

Shape the mixture into 12 patties. Brush with melted butter and arrange on a greased double-hinged wire grill. Place on rack 6 inches over heat and grill 20 to 30 minutes, turning and basting several times with butter.

Serves 6–12.

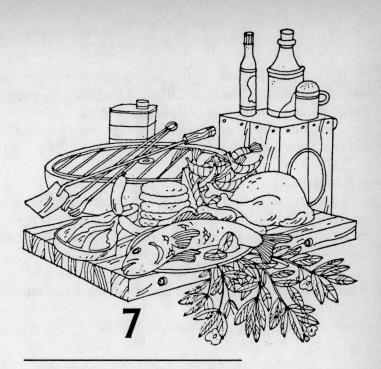

7

Foil Cookery

ALL THROUGH the South Pacific, the Caribbean, much of Africa, and most of the tropical lands around the world, it is customary to wrap foods in large, flavorsome leaves and cook them in the smoldering embers of dying fires. The natural moisture of the leaves, such as those from banana plants, prevents the foods from burning; of course, the fires should be very low and banked, without visible flames, or the food will scorch. I've learned by experience that almost identical results can be obtained if the foods to be cooked are wrapped in heavy-duty aluminum foil to substitute for the leaves.

Once again, be sure to use heavy-duty aluminum foil; wrap the packets of food carefully and seal the edges so the juices remain within the foil packages. As an added plus, consider this: there's no cleaning up afterward, because the foil is thrown away after being used.

FOIL WRAPPING

To make an airtight package (when all liquid must be prevented from evaporating), place food on foil cut to size. Bring long edges of foil together, up and over the food; fold over twice to seal. Double-fold each end of packet.

It's not always necessary to seal tightly. Even when foil is just loosely folded over food, flavor and much moisture are held in.

Chicken in Papers, Singapore Style

4 whole chicken breasts
½ cup soy sauce
3 tablespoons vegetable oil
1½ cups chopped mushrooms
¾ cup chopped scallions
⅓ cup chopped water chestnuts
1 teaspoon salt
½ teaspoon freshly ground black pepper
½ teaspoon powdered ginger
¼ teaspoon cinnamon
1 tablespoon dry sherry

Cut the chicken breasts in half through the breastbone. Remove the skin and bones. Cut each piece in half to make it thinner. Put the breasts between two sheets of wax paper and pound them as thin as possible. Marinate chicken in ⅓ cup of soy sauce for 1 hour.

Meanwhile, heat oil in a skillet; sauté mushrooms, scallions, and water chestnuts for 5 minutes, stirring frequently. Mix in remaining soy sauce, seasonings, and sherry. Cool.

Spread equal amounts of the mixture on one side of each chicken breast. Fold over and press edges together firmly. Wrap each breast in greased aluminum foil, sealing the edges.

Arrange the packets on a greased rack and grill 4 inches over heat for 20 minutes, turning the packets to cook both sides. Fold back foil to serve.

Serves 8.

Note: Smaller versions make excellent hors d'oeuvre. Cut the pounded chicken into squares and proceed as directed, but cook only 10 minutes.

Pecan-Stuffed Chicken Breasts, Southern Style

4 whole chicken breasts
4 teaspoons salt
1 teaspoon freshly ground black pepper
¼ cup lemon juice
¼ pound (1 stick) butter, melted
3 cups toasted breadcrumbs

1 cup coarsely chopped pecans
¼ cup hot chicken broth
½ cup chopped sautéed celery
½ cup chopped sautéed onion

Cut each chicken breast in half through the breastbone. Rinse and dry. Sprinkle with half the salt and pepper, then brush with lemon juice and 3 tablespoons of the butter.

Mix breadcrumbs and nuts. Stir in broth, then celery, onion, and the remaining salt and pepper. Cut 8 pieces of heavy-duty aluminum foil, each about 12 inches long. Place a mound of the dressing on each center, then place a chicken breast on each mound. Fold the foil over the chicken, sealing the edges completely.

Arrange on a grill 5 inches over heat and grill 25 to 30 minutes, turning the packages several times. To serve, unfold the foil and turn out, stuffing side down, onto heated platter. Serves 8.

Lamb Chops in Foil, Greek Style

8 loin or shoulder lamb chops, 2 inches thick
1½ teaspoons salt
½ teaspoon freshly ground black pepper
2 cloves garlic, minced
½ teaspoon crumbled thyme
½ teaspoon crumbled oregano
½ pound feta cheese, crumbled

Rinse and dry the chops. Cut 8 pieces of heavy-duty aluminum foil 12 inches long. Lightly oil the foil and put a chop in center of each. Mix all remaining ingredients and divide the mixture evenly among the chops, coating the tops. Fold up foil, sealing the edges completely.

Arrange the packages on a grill 5 inches over the heat. Grill 30 minutes. To serve, fold back foil. Serves 8.

Lamb Shanks, Yugoslavian Style

6 lamb shanks
½ cup olive oil
½ cup red wine vinegar
2 teaspoons salt
¾ teaspoon freshly ground black pepper
2 cloves garlic, minced
½ teaspoon oregano

Crack the shanks in two places; rinse and dry. Put the shanks in a glass or stainless steel baking pan, large enough for a single layer.

Mix all remaining ingredients and pour over shanks. Cover and marinate overnight in the refrigerator or 3 hours at room temperature. Drain.

Cut 6 pieces of heavy-duty aluminum foil large enough to completely enfold the shanks. Place a shank on each and spoon a little marinade over. Fold up the foil, sealing the edges carefully. Place on the grill 4 inches over heat and cook 1 hour, turning the packets several times. Unwrap the shanks and place directly on the grill. Grill until browned on all sides, about 5 minutes.

Serves 6.

Armenian Lamb and Vegetable Melange

2 pounds boneless shoulder of lamb
1 eggplant, cut lengthwise into 8 pieces
2 tomatoes, quartered
2 onions, quartered
2 green peppers, quartered and seeded
2 potatoes, peeled and quartered
2 teaspoons salt
¾ teaspoon freshly ground black pepper
½ teaspoon crumbled thyme

Cut the lamb into 4 pieces. Cut 4 pieces of heavy-duty aluminum foil 12 inches long. Put a piece of lamb in the center of each. Divide vegetables equally over lamb pieces; season with salt, pepper, and thyme. Fold over foil, sealing the edges. Place packets on a rack 6 inches over heat and grill 2 hours. To serve, unwrap and turn out onto plates.

Serves 4.

Barbecued Pork, Georgian Style

1 6-pound leg of pork	1 tablespoon
1 tablespoon salt	Worcestershire sauce
¾ teaspoon freshly ground	½ teaspoon dry mustard
black pepper	3 tablespoons olive oil
2 teaspoons minced garlic	1 tablespoon cider vinegar
1 teaspoon minced ginger	1 cup chopped peanuts
	1 cup boiling water

Rinse and dry pork. Prick the leg in several places. Rub with a mixture of salt, pepper, garlic, and ginger. Let stand 1 hour.

Cut a piece of heavy-duty aluminum foil large enough to completely enfold the leg. Place the leg on it and bring up the edges, closing them loosely. Place on a rack 4 inches over heat. Roast 1½ hours, turning leg twice. Mix together remaining ingredients. Open the foil and pour the mixture over the pork, basting several times. Close foil, and roast 2 hours longer, basting occasionally.

Transfer pork to a heated serving dish and carefully pour gravy into saucepan. Skim the fat and taste for seasoning. Reheat when ready to serve. Carve thin slices.

Serves 10–12.

Pork Chops with Black Bean Sauce

6 pork chops, 1½ inches	4 green onions, minced
thick	2 cloves garlic, minced
1 teaspoon Chinese five-	¼ cup dry sherry
spice powder	2 tablespoons soy sauce
1 teaspoon salt	¼ cup beef broth
3 tablespoons Chinese	
salted black beans	

Rinse and dry the pork chops, then rub with the five-spice powder and salt.

Soak black beans in cold water for 15 minutes. Drain, rinse, and drain again. Mash beans with green onions and garlic; mix in remaining ingredients.

Cut 6 pices of heavy-duty aluminum foil large enough to completely enfold the chops. Place a chop on each piece and spoon bean mixture over each. Fold foil together, sealing the edges together carefully. Place the packets on a rack 5 inches above heat. Grill, turning packets several times with tongs, for 45 minutes. To serve, fold back foil.

Serves 6.

Swiss Steak

3 pounds chuck steak, 1 inch thick
3 teaspoons salt
1 teaspoon freshly ground black pepper
¼ cup vegetable oil
1 cup minced onions
½ cup chopped green pepper

½ pound mushrooms, sliced
2 tablespoons flour
1 16-ounce can tomatoes, drained
2 tablespoons steak sauce
Chopped parsley

Cut steak into 8 pieces. Season with 2 teaspoons of salt and ½ teaspoon pepper.

Heat oil in a skillet. Sauté the onions and green peppers 10 minutes, stirring frequently. Add mushrooms; cook 2 minutes. Blend in flour and remaining salt and pepper. Add tomatoes, stirring until mixture boils. Mix in the steak sauce.

Cut 8 14-inch squares of heavy-duty aluminum foil. Grease the centers and place a piece of steak on each. Bring foil up around the steaks and spread the sauce over them. Close the foil and double fold the edges to seal tightly. Place on grill 4 inches over heat and cook 1 hour, turning the packages with tongs several times. Serve with the foil folded back, garnished with parsley.

Serves 8.

Fillets of Fish with Green Sauce, Dalmatian Style

4 anchovies	4 tablespoons chopped onion
½ cup French-style mustard	¼ cup finely chopped parsley
½ cup olive oil	6 fillets of sole or snapper
¼ cup lemon juice	2 teaspoons salt
1 tablespoon vinegar	¾ teaspoon freshly ground black pepper
½ cup finely chopped dill pickles	

In blender container, combine anchovies, mustard, oil, lemon juice, and vinegar. Blend until smooth. Mix in pickles, onion, and parsley. Blend 1 second.

Rinse and dry the fish; season with salt and pepper. Cut 6 pieces of heavy-duty aluminum foil large enough to enfold the fillets completely. Grease foil and put a fillet on each piece. Spread 1 tablespoon of sauce on each fillet. Fold up foil, sealing the edges. Place on grill 4 inches above heat. Grill 20 minutes, turning packages once with tongs. Open packets, fold back foil, and serve with the remaining sauce.

Serves 6.

Fish Goulash in Foil, Hungarian Style

6 fish steaks, 1 inch thick
3 teaspoons salt
1 teaspoon white pepper
2 tablespoons paprika
1 pound potatoes, peeled
   and sliced thin
2 tomatoes, sliced thin

¼ pound mushrooms,
   sliced thin
1 green pepper, seeded
   and cut into thin
   strips
½ cup sour cream
3 tablespoons butter

Buy whitefish, salmon, or striped bass in 1-inch steaks. Wash and dry the fish; rub with half the salt and pepper and 2 teaspoons of paprika.

Cut 6 pieces of heavy-duty aluminum foil 12 inches long. Put a fish steak in the center of each and cover with an equal amount of potatoes, tomatoes, mushrooms, and green pepper.

Mix sour cream with remaining salt, pepper, and paprika. Spread over vegetables. Place a pat of butter on top; bring up the foil and seal the edges carefully.

Place on a grill 4 inches over heat and grill 20 to 25 minutes, turning the packets several times. To serve, fold back foil.

Serves 6.

Spiced Fish in Papers, Cambodian Style

2 pounds fillets of sole
½ pound raw shrimp,
   shelled and deveined
½ cup chopped scallions
2 cloves garlic, minced

1 teaspoon salt
¼ teaspoon Tabasco
1 teaspoon anchovy paste
3 tablespoons dry white
   wine

Rinse and dry the fillets; cut into bite-sized pieces. Add all remaining ingredients and mix lightly but thoroughly.

Cut 8 pieces of heavy-duty aluminum foil about 8 inches long. Lightly oil each piece. Divide the mixture evenly onto foil pieces. Fold envelope style and seal edges of packets. Place on rack 5 inches over the heat and cook 15 to 20 minutes, turning the envelopes with tongs to cook all sides. Fold back the foil to serve.

Serves 8.

Minced Fish in Foil, Malaysian Style

2 pounds fish fillets
¾ cup grated packaged
    coconut
    (unsweetened if
    possible)
3 tablespoons butter
¾ cup chopped onions
2 cloves garlic, minced

2 eggs, beaten
¼ cup ground cashew nuts
1½ teaspoons salt
1 tablespoon curry
    powder
½ cup heavy cream
Vegetable oil

Wash the fish, and process in a food processor or chop or grind very fine.

If the coconut is sweetened, rinse it under cold water, drain, and dry. Melt butter in a skillet; sauté coconut until lightly browned. Watch carefully to prevent burning. Combine with fish; add the onions, garlic, eggs, cashew nuts, salt, curry powder, and cream. Process again, or chop until smooth and fine.

Cut 8 8-inch squares of heavy-duty aluminum foil and oil lightly. Divide the mixture among the squares and fold envelope fashion, sealing the center and ends. Place on rack

5 inches above heat and cook 30 minutes, turning with tongs to cook all sides. Fold back foil to serve.

Serves 8.

Note: Smaller versions make excellent hors d'oeuvre.

Stuffed Fish, Cuban Style

1 4-pound mackerel, snapper, or cod	2 tablespoons minced onion
3 teaspoons salt	1 clove garlic, minced
1 teaspoon freshly ground black pepper	2 raw eggs, beaten
2 tablespoons lemon juice	¼ cup chopped seedless raisins
3 cups fresh breadcrumbs	½ cup chopped pimento-stuffed olives
½ cup bottled clam juice	
3 hard-cooked eggs, chopped	

Use a whole fish or a center cut of cod. Split and bone the fish. Season with 2 teaspoons of salt and ⅓ teaspoon of pepper; add lemon juice.

Soak breadcrumbs in the clam juice, then mix in chopped eggs, onion, garlic, raw eggs, raisins, olives, and remaining salt and pepper. Stuff the fish and secure the opening with skewers or thread.

Wrap the fish securely in heavy-duty aluminum foil. Place on rack 5 inches above heat. Grill about 45 minutes, turning the packet frequently with tongs. To test doneness, fold back foil and test with a fork. If a fish flakes easily, it is done.

Serves 6–8.

Salmon in Foil, Alaskan Style

1 5-pound whole salmon
   or a similar weight
   cut from a large
   salmon
1 tablespoon salt
1 teaspoon freshly ground
   white pepper

1 lemon, thinly sliced
1 onion, thinly sliced
12 dill or parsley sprigs
   Oil

If a whole salmon is used, remove the head. Split the salmon (either whole or section), but do not separate. Wash and dry. Sprinkle inside and out with salt and pepper, then spread lemon and onion slices and dill in the cavity. Close fish. Wrap the fish in a double layer of oiled heavy-duty aluminum foil, bringing the edges together and sealing the center and ends of packet.

Place the package on rack 6 inches over heat. Grill 45 minutes, turning the package several times. Fold back the foil at the center fold and make a cut in the thickest part of the fish. If it flakes easily and is not translucent, it's done—if not, cover again and cook until it is. Serve with dill sauce if desired.

Serves 8–12.

Trout in Foil, Polynesian Style

6 small brook trout
3 tablespoons soy sauce
⅓ cup vegetable oil
¼ cup lemon juice

1 teaspoon ground ginger
½ pound fresh spinach,
   washed and dried

If possible, buy fresh trout, then remove the heads and wash and dry. (Thaw frozen trout according to directions on package.)

Mix together soy sauce, oil, lemon juice, and ginger. Brush mixture on fish, inside and out. Let stand 1 hour.

Cut 6 pieces of heavy-duty aluminum foil large enough to completely enfold the fish. Spread some spinach leaves in the center of each piece of foil. Put a fish on the spinach and cover with additional spinach. Fold up foil, sealing edges carefully. Place on grill 5 inches over heat and grill 20 to 25 minutes, turning packets several times. Roll back foil and serve.

Serves 6.

8

Spit Roasting

THROUGHOUT the Balkans and Middle East, a familiar sight in front of restaurants is that of a whole lamb being roasted on a spit. Every few minutes someone turns the spit. We don't have that problem—electric or battery-operated spits have taken the work out of spit cooking.

Always follow the manufacturer's instructions for operating your grill. Here are some general rules.

EQUIPMENT NEEDED

Barbecue or grill
Spit to hold the meat or poultry
Metal spit forks to secure the food
Electric or battery-operated rotisserie motor
Charcoal

When the equipment is assembled, use the desired number of charcoal briquets and spread them out so that they will extend four inches beyond the length of the food to be cooked. About six inches is a good width. (The number of briquets needed will be about thirty-six. See Chapter 2 for instructions about starting the fire.) Add more briquets to the top of the burning ones, about every two inches. Put the food on the spit and turn the motor on. Place a drip pan or aluminum foil on the rack underneath the food. Follow instructions in individual recipes for basting. Add more briquets from time to time (about every thirty minutes) to maintain heat.

If the barbecue has a hood or cover, turn the open side away from the wind. An open-spit barbecue should be kept in a protected area.

POSITIONING THE FOOD TO BE COOKED

If you can't judge the center of the food to be cooked with your eye, use a ruler. Insert the spit in the meat. To test the balance, put the ends of the spit (with the food on it) in the palms of your hands, and try rolling the spit. If the spit doesn't turn easily, move the spit or use a balance weight— a necessary and easily obtainable accessory. Be sure that poultry wings are tied to the body of the bird. Boned meat should be tied too.

THERMOMETERS

Although times for cooking are given in each recipe, a thermometer is the most accurate guide to the degree of doneness of large cuts of meat and poultry. For meat, insert it in the thickest part of the meat, but not touching any bone. For poultry, insert it in the thickest part of the breast, but not touching any bone.

The recipes that follow may also be prepared in the oven on a spit for year-round enjoyment.

Capon on a Spit, Italian Style

1 7-pound capon	¾ teaspoon freshly ground
½ lemon	black pepper
12 sprigs fresh basil (see	¼ pound (1 stick) butter,
note)	softened
2½ teaspoons salt	½ cup dry red wine

Wash, clean, and dry the capon. Truss, tying the wings close to the body. Rub inside and out with lemon, then place 2 sprigs of basil in the cavity. Chop remaining basil. Rub capon inside and out with salt and pepper.

Blend half the butter and all but 1 teaspoon of the basil and rub all over the capon. Spit the bird securely and place drip pan underneath. Roast 3 to 3½ hours, basting frequently with a mixture of wine and remaining butter and basil. Let stand 20 minutes before carving.

Serves 6–8.

Note: If fresh basil is not available, use 1 tablespoon dried. Rub the interior with a little and use the rest with the butter.

Stuffed Capon, Kashmir Style

1 6-pound capon	6 tablespoons melted butter
3 teaspoons salt	2 cups chopped onions
1 teaspoon freshly ground black pepper	2 teaspoons ground coriander seeds
6 cardamom seeds, ground (out of pods)	¾ pound ground lamb
1 teaspoon turmeric	1 cup yogurt
	1½ teaspoons chili powder

Wash and dry the capon. Prick the skin. Mix 2 teaspoons of the salt, the pepper, cardamom, and turmeric. Rub capon with mixture inside and outside. Let stand while preparing stuffing.

Heat 4 tablespoons of butter in a skillet; sauté onions for 10 minutes. Mix coriander, lamb, and remaining salt. Cook, stirring almost constantly, until lamb is lightly browned. Cool. Stuff the capon with mixture; close the opening with skewers and truss. Spit the capon securely and arrange on grill. Place a drip pan beneath. Roast 3 to 3½ hours, basting with the yogurt mixed with the chili powder and remaining butter.

Serves 6–8.

Greek Oregano Chicken

1 5-pound roasting chicken	¼ cup lemon juice
½ cup dry red wine	1 teaspoon oregano
2 teaspoons salt	¼ cup olive oil
½ teaspoon freshly ground black pepper	

Wash, clean, and dry the chicken. Mix wine, salt, pepper, lemon juice, and oregano. Rub into chicken, inside and out;

let stand 1 hour. Drain and mix the marinade with oil. Put the chicken on a spit with a drip pan underneath. Roast 2½ to 3 hours, basting frequently with the marinade mixture. Serves 4.

Chicken Tandoor

2 2-pound broiling chickens, whole	⅛ teaspoon ground anise seed
2 teaspoons salt	1 teaspoon ground cumin seed
¼ cup lime or lemon juice	
1 tablespoon minced garlic	½ teaspoon red vegetable food coloring
2 tablespoons chopped ginger root	2 cups unflavored yogurt
2 tablespoons ground coriander seeds	3 tablespoons vegetable oil
	Lime sections
¼ teaspoon cayenne pepper	Chopped onion

Carefully pull skin off the chickens. Prick chickens all over and rub meat with salt and lime or lemon juice. Let stand for 30 minutes. Make parallel gashes in the chicken every inch or so. Place in a large bowl.

Combine garlic, seasonings, food coloring, and ¼ cup of the yogurt in an electric blender. Blend until smooth, then combine with remaining yogurt. Brush the chickens inside and out with the yogurt mixture. Cover and refrigerate overnight.

When ready to cook, spit the chickens securely. Check the balance. Put a drip pan underneath. Brush with oil and cook 2 to 2½ hours, or until chickens are tender. Quarter the chickens and serve with lime sections and chopped onion. Serves 4–6.

Indian Chicken on the Spit

1 3-pound chicken
1½ teaspoons salt
½ teaspoon freshly ground
    black pepper
1 teaspoon cumin seed,
    crushed

1 cup minced onions
2 cloves garlic, minced
¼ pound (1 stick) butter,
    melted

Wash and dry the chicken. Mix salt, pepper, cumin, onions, and garlic. Chop or pound the mixture to a paste; rub thoroughly into the chicken. Let stand 1 hour. Put chicken on spit, being careful to balance properly. Place a drip pan under it and baste bird with melted butter. Cook 1 hour, or until leg bone moves easily, basting frequently with the melted butter. Thermometer should register 185° F.

If you don't have a spit, have the chicken split or quartered. Prepare as directed, then put in a double-hinged wire grill and broil 35 to 45 minutes, basting and turning frequently. Serves 4.

Spiced Chicken, Chinese Style

2 2½-pound broiling
    chickens, whole
2½ teaspoons salt
½ teaspoon freshly ground
    black pepper
2 teaspoons sugar
1 tablespoon minced
    garlic

2 teaspoons Chinese five-
    spice powder
½ cup soy sauce
3 tablespoons vegetable
    oil

Wash and dry the chicken. Mix all remaining ingredients and brush on chickens, inside and out. Let stand 2 hours. Spit the chickens securely with a drip pan underneath. Cook 1½ hours, or until tender. Cut into small pieces.

Serves 4–8.

Note: If you prefer, the chickens may be split and grilled for 30 minutes.

Thai Roast Chicken

1 5-pound roasting chicken	1 teaspoon crushed
1 cup soy sauce	coriander seeds
2 tablespoons dry sherry	2 cloves garlic, minced
1 teaspoon salt	

Wash, clean, and dry the chicken. Combine all remaining ingredients and brush on chicken, inside and out. Let stand 1 hour. Drain, reserving marinade. Secure chicken on spit with drip pan underneath. Roast 2 to 3 hours, or until tender, basting frequently with marinade.

Serves 4.

Note: If you like, the chicken may be cut into quarters and grilled. If so, reduce cooking time to 1 hour.

Curried Duck, Burmese Style

1 5-pound duck	3 tablespoons curry
2 teaspoons salt	powder
½ teaspoon freshly ground	¼ teaspoon dried ground
black pepper	red peppers
3 cloves garlic, minced	

Clean, wash, and dry the duck. Remove as much fat as possible. Mix together all remaining ingredients and rub the paste into the duck, inside and out. Let stand at room temperature 2 hours or refrigerate overnight.

Truss the duck, and spit securely with drip pan underneath. Roast 2 hours, pricking the skin frequently to permit fat to run out.

Serves 2–4.

Roast Goose, Bohemian Style

1 10-pound goose	2 teaspoons paprika
12 cloves garlic	3 tablespoons minced
1 tablespoon salt	garlic
1 teaspoon freshly ground black pepper	Applesauce

Clean, wash, and dry the goose. Remove as much fat as possible. Prick the skin all over without puncturing the meat. Peel and crush garlic cloves; place in the cavity of the bird.

Mix salt, pepper, paprika, and minced garlic. Rub inside and out. Truss the goose. Let stand 2 hours at room temperature. Secure the goose on the spit with a drip pan underneath. Roast 3½ to 4 hours, or until tender and juices are no longer pink when goose is pricked with a fork. Baste frequently with pan drippings. Serve with applesauce.

Serves 6–8.

Iranian Leg of Lamb

1 5–6-pound leg of lamb,
   boned, rolled, and
   tied
1 teaspoon coriander
   seeds, crushed
½ teaspoon freshly ground
   black pepper

¾ cup minced onions
2 cloves garlic, minced
1 cup yogurt
¼ cup melted butter

Wash and dry the lamb; make shallow gashes in meat.

Mix coriander, pepper, onions, and garlic until a paste is formed. Mix in yogurt. Coat lamb with mixture and let stand 2 hours.

Secure lamb on a spit with drip pan underneath. Roast 2½ hours (meat thermometer should register 180° F.), basting with melted butter and remaining yogurt mixture.

Serves 6–8.

Rack of Lamb, Italian Style

1 rack of lamb (2–3
   pounds)
2 teaspoons salt
¾ teaspoon freshly ground
   black pepper

½ teaspoon rosemary
3 cloves garlic, slivered

Wrap the bone ends of the ribs in foil, or put a cube of potato on them. Rub the lamb with salt, pepper, and rosemary. Make tiny slits in lamb and insert garlic in slits. Let stand 2 hours.

Spit lamb securely, and roast 30 minutes (140° F. on a meat thermometer). Cut into ribs or carve in narrow, thin slices lengthwise.

Serves 2–4.

Roast Leg of Lamb, Lebanese Style

1 6-pound leg of lamb	1 teaspoon crumbled
2 cloves garlic	oregano
2½ teaspoons salt	½ cup lemon juice
1 teaspoon freshly ground	½ cup ouzo (licorice-
black pepper	flavored liquor)

Wash and dry the leg of lamb. Make about 10 incisions in the flat side of lamb. Peel garlic and cut into 10 slivers; insert in the incisions.

Combine salt, pepper, and oregano and rub all over the lamb. Spit leg securely and place on rotisserie with drip pan underneath. For rare lamb, roast 1½ hours (to 140° F. on a meat thermometer), basting frequently with a mixture of lemon juice and ouzo. After half an hour or so, baste with the drippings. Remove lamb and let stand 15 minutes. Carve into slices.

Serves 10–12.

Rolled Leg of Lamb, Italian Style

1 5-pound leg of lamb	1 teaspoon oregano
2 teaspoons salt	2 cloves garlic, minced
1 teaspoon freshly ground	Olive oil
black pepper	

Have the butcher bone, roll, and tie the leg. Mix salt, pepper, oregano, and garlic. Make about 6 small slits in the meat. Rub meat with herb mixture, forcing a little into the slits.

Secure meat on the spit and brush with olive oil. Put a drip pan underneath. Roast 1½ hours for pink meat. If you prefer medium or well done, grill until meat thermometer registers 175° F., about 2½ hours. Serve in thin slices.

Serves 6–8.

Spiced Lamb, Indian Style

3 pounds boneless lamb, in 1 piece
1 cup chopped onions
2 tablespoons coriander seeds
1 teaspoon freshly ground black pepper

2 teaspoons salt
½ teaspoon ground ginger
1 cup yogurt
4 tablespoons melted butter

Wash and dry the lamb. In the container of a blender, combine all remaining ingredients. Blend until smooth. Marinate lamb in mixture 2 hours; drain, reserving marinade.

Spit lamb securely with a drip pan underneath. Roast 45 to 55 minutes, brushing frequently with marinade. Serve in thin slices.

Serves 6–8.

Spit-Roasted Lamb, Hawaiian Style

1 6-pound leg of lamb, boned and tied
2 cloves garlic, minced
1 teaspoon salt

¾ cup dry red wine
¾ cup pineapple juice
¾ cup soy sauce
½ cup gin

Rinse and dry the lamb; make several small gashes in the surface. Place in a bowl. Mix together all remaining ingredients. Pour over lamb and marinate overnight in the refrigerator, basting several times. Drain lamb, reserving marinade.

Spit the lamb securely with a drip pan underneath. Roast for 1¾ hours for medium-rare meat, 2½ hours for well done. Brush frequently with marinade.

Serves 8–12.

Stuffed Spiced Lamb, Indonesian Style

4 pounds boned leg or
shoulder of lamb,
pounded thin
3 cups chopped onions
8 cloves garlic, minced
2 teaspoons salt
1 teaspoon freshly ground
black pepper
½ teaspoon dried ground
red pepper

4 teaspoons ground cumin
seeds
1 green pepper, seeded
and minced
2 sweet red peppers,
seeded and minced
Melted butter

Rinse and dry the lamb. Combine remaining ingredients except butter; spread mixture over ⅔ of lamb. Roll up like a jelly roll, and tie with string in several places. Spit the lamb securely with a drip pan in the bottom of the grill. Cook 1½ hours, basting frequently with melted butter. Let stand for 15 minutes before slicing.

Serves 8–10.

Mock Venison, German Style

1 6-pound leg or shoulder of mutton	1 tablespoon salt
2 cups dry red wine	1 teaspoon freshly ground black pepper
1 cup wine vinegar	1 teaspoon thyme
½ cup orange juice	1 bay leaf
1 cup sliced onions	½ cup olive oil
3 cloves garlic, minced	

Start this dish 2 or 3 days in advance.

Tie the mutton securely. In a large pan or glass or pottery bowl, mix all remaining ingredients. Pour over meat and marinate meat well covered in mixture in the refrigerator for at least 48 hours.

When ready to cook, drain, reserving marinade. Spit meat securely with drip pan underneath. Roast 2½ hours, until meat thermometer registers 175° F.

Skim fat from drippings and combine drippings with marinade. Bring to a boil and cook over low heat 10 minutes. Thicken with a little arrowroot or cornstarch. Serve in a sauceboat.

Serves 8–10.

Barbecued Pork, Fijian Style

8 pounds pork loin	1 cup water
3 teaspoons salt	1 6-ounce can frozen pineapple juice, thawed
1 cup orange marmalade	
¼ cup prepared mustard	
¼ cup Worcestershire sauce	

Crack the bones between the ribs of the pork loin. Rub pork with salt. Mix remaining ingredients; pour mixture over pork and let stand for 2 hours at room temperature, basting several times.

Drain pork, reserving the marinade. Spit pork securely with a drip pan underneath. Roast 3½ hours, or until no pink shows in center, basting frequently with marinade. Carve pork into individual ribs.

Serves 6–8.

Chinese Barbecued Loin of Pork

1 8-rib pork loin

Bone the pork and marinate for 4 hours at room temperature or overnight in the refrigerator, basting and turning several times in one of the following mixtures:

SOY	PINEAPPLE
1 cup soy sauce	1 cup pineapple juice
½ cup dry sherry	¾ cup soy sauce
3 tablespoons honey	½ cup dry sherry
1 teaspoon salt	2 cloves garlic, minced
2 cloves garlic, minced	2 tablespoons brown sugar

Drain pork and spit securely with drip pan underneath. Roast 30 minutes per pound, basting frequently with marinade. You may also place it on a rack, about 6 inches over heat, and grill 30 minutes a pound, turning several times and basting each turn. In either case, no pink should show in center. Slice thin.

Serves 8–10.

Cinnamon Pork, Indonesian Style

4 pounds pork loin, boned and tied	¾ teaspoon freshly ground black pepper
2 tablespoons minced garlic	2 tablespoons soy sauce
½ cup grated onion	2 teaspoons sugar
2 teaspoons salt	2 tablespoons cinnamon

Rinse and dry the pork; make small cuts all over surface of meat.

Mix all remaining ingredients. Rub all over pork, forcing some of mixture into cuts. Let stand 2 hours.

Spit the pork securely with drip pan underneath. Roast 2 hours, basting several times with pan drippings. Carve thin slices; serve with hot mustard.

Serves 8–12.

Loin of Pork, Italian Style

1 8-rib pork loin	¼ cup olive oil
2 teaspoons salt	2 cloves garlic, minced
¾ teaspoon freshly ground black pepper	½ teaspoon oregano
1½ cups dry red wine	2 bay leaves

Rub pork with salt and pepper. Mix all remaining ingredients. Marinate pork in mixture overnight in refrigerator, basting frequently. Drain, reserving marinade.

Spit pork securely with drip pan underneath. Grill 30 minutes per pound, until no pink shows in center. Brush frequently with marinade.

Serves 6–8.

Malaysian Pork Loin

1 6-pound pork loin
2 teaspoons salt
¾ teaspoon freshly ground
    black pepper
2 teaspoons ground
    coriander seeds
1 teaspoon ground cumin
    seeds
1 teaspoon ground ginger
½ teaspoon saffron
2 cloves garlic, minced

Cut the rib bones short. Prick the pork in several places. Combine all remaining ingredients; rub mixture into pork. Cover and let stand 1 hour.

Secure pork on the spit with drip pan beneath. Roast 3 hours until no pink shows in center, basting occasionally with pan drippings. Let stand 15 minutes before carving. Serves 8–10.

Puerto Rican Orange Pork

1 6-pound pork loin
2 teaspoons salt
¾ teaspoon freshly ground
    black pepper
2 6-ounce cans frozen
    orange juice, thawed
1½ cups water
2 teaspoons
    minced garlic
1½ teaspoons oregano
2 tablespoons olive oil
½ cup currant jelly
1½ cups dry white wine

Cut gashes between the ribs of the pork. Rub pork with salt and pepper and place in bowl.

Combine in a saucepan orange juice, water, garlic, oregano, and oil. Bring to a boil and pour over pork. Let stand at room temperature 2 hours, basting several times.

Drain pork; secure on spit with drip pan beneath. Roast 3 hours or until no pink shows in center. Baste frequently

with the marinade. Combine the jelly and wine in a saucepan with the drippings. Bring to a boil and cook over low heat 10 minutes. Carve the pork and serve jelly sauce in a sauceboat.
Serves 6–8.

Uruguayan Marinated Roast Pork

1 8-pound pork loin
1 tablespoon coarse salt
2 tablespoons minced garlic
2 teaspoons thyme
1 teaspoon powdered bay leaves
¼ teaspoon Tabasco
½ cup red wine vinegar
¼ cup olive oil

Sponge and dry pork. Cut gashes near rib bones. Mix all remaining ingredients; rub mixture into pork. Place in a container, cover, and let stand in the refrigerator for 2 or more hours.

Secure pork on a spit with drip pan beneath. Roast for 30 minutes per pound, or until no pink shows in center. Carve and serve hot.
Serves 8.

Australian Roast Beef

1 3-rib roast beef (about 6 pounds, trimmed weight)
1 teaspoon thyme
1 teaspoon freshly ground black pepper
1 cup dry red wine
2 tablespoons brandy
Salt

Cut the rib bones down very short, and use for another purpose. Rub the meat with thyme and pepper. Place in a bowl; pour a mixture of wine and brandy over the meat. Let stand 1 hour. Drain, reserving marinade.

Secure meat on spit with a drip pan underneath. Roast 1¾ hours for rare meat, 2 for medium, 2½ for well done. Baste several times with marinade. Remove from heat and sprinkle with salt. Let stand 15 minutes before carving.

Serves 6–8.

Rotisserie Roast Beef

Two or three ribs may be roasted on a rotisserie. Cut the bones very short and tie meat securely. Insert spit diagonally so it balances the meat properly. Insert meat thermometer as close to the center as possible, being sure it doesn't touch the spit or bones. Roast until thermometer registers 130° F. for rare, 140° F. for medium, or 160° F. for well done. If you don't have a thermometer, allow 15 minutes per pound for rare, 18 for medium, and 22 for well done.

Australian Spit-Roasted Turkey

1 10–12-pound turkey	½ cup dry white wine
1 tablespoon salt	1 tablespoon chopped
¾ teaspoon freshly ground	chives
black pepper	¼ cup minced parsley
½ cup vegetable oil	1 teaspoon sage

Clean, wash, and dry the turkey. Rub inside and out with salt and pepper. Tie wings close to the body and the drumsticks together. Spit turkey securely and arrange on motorized spit. Place a drip pan underneath. Cook 2½ hours, brushing frequently with mixture of remaining ingredients. Meat thermometer should register 185° F. Remove from spit and let stand 20 minutes before carving.

Serves 10–12.

Barbecued Suckling Pig, Bulgarian Style

A suckling pig tastes best when 4 to 6 weeks old. Be sure to handle the pig gently, so as not to tear the skin.

1 suckling pig, 8 to 10 pounds	1 cup chopped walnuts
½ cup olive oil	1 teaspoon sage
1 pound butter	1 teaspoon thyme
1 cup chopped onions	½ teaspoon nutmeg
1 cup chopped celery	6 eggs, beaten lightly
6 pork sausages, sliced	Salt
½ pound bacon, cooked, drained, and crumbled	Freshly ground black pepper
6 cups crumbled corn bread	1 bottle steak sauce

Sponge pig with olive oil. Melt 4 tablespoons butter in a skillet; sauté onions and celery 10 minutes, stirring frequently. Remove from pan. Brown sausages and drain.

Mix together sautéed vegetables, sausage, bacon, corn bread, walnuts, sage, thyme, nutmeg, eggs, and salt and pepper to taste.

Stuff the pig loosely and close opening securely with skewers. (Bake surplus stuffing, if any, in a greased casserole for 45 minutes in a 350° F. oven.) Insert spit rod through opening of pig, being careful to balance properly. Place the smaller prongs in the body and bolt securely. Arrange the revolving spit over the coals with drip pan beneath.

Melt remaining butter and stir in steak sauce. Roast the pig 25 minutes per pound, or until no pink shows in center, basting frequently with sauce.

Serves 8–10.

Hawaiian Turkey

1 10–12-pound turkey	1½ cups water
1 tablespoon salt	⅔ cup firmly packed
½ teaspoon freshly ground	brown sugar
black pepper	¾ cup wine vinegar
2 6-ounce cans frozen	½ cup honey
pineapple juice,	
thawed	

Clean, wash, and dry the turkey. Rub inside and out with salt and pepper. Mix all remaining ingredients.

Put turkey on spit with a drip pan underneath. Roast 1½ hours, basting frequently with sauce. Heat remaining sauce and serve in a sauceboat to pour on carved turkey. Sautéed canned pineapple slices and baked yams or sweet potatoes are good accompaniments.

Serves 10–12.

Peruvian Barbecued Turkey

1 10-pound turkey
2 cloves garlic, minced
2 teaspoons salt
¾ teaspoon freshly ground
   black pepper
1 teaspoon hickory-smoked
   salt

1 teaspoon crumbled
   oregano
½ teaspoon ground cumin
   seed
¼ pound (1 stick) butter,
   softened

Clean, wash, and dry the turkey. Loosen the skin of the breast very carefully, forming a pocket. Rub turkey inside and out with garlic, salt, and pepper.

Blend hickory salt, oregano, and cumin into butter. Spread half the mixture in the breast pocket; pat skin in place. Cover and chill 3 hours.

Truss the turkey, and fasten securely on the spit with a drip pan underneath. Cook 2¼ hours, brushing frequently with remaining butter mixture.

Serves 10–12.

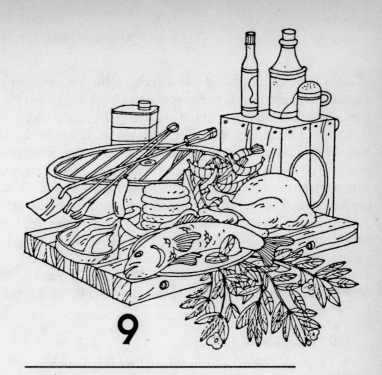

9

Hibachi Cooking

HIBACHIS originated in Japan. They are small, heavy metal grills chiefly used in Japan, but also in Korea; the heat radiates from beneath, and the grill itself is comparatively small and compact. In effect, they are tabletop models of the outdoor charcoal or electric grills popular in our country.

Hibachis can readily be used on top of tables, providing the surface beneath the grill is heatproof. For this reason, the hibachi should be placed on a metal table or tabletop to prevent possible damage. Everyone can cook his or her own food, which certainly should enliven the gathering and bring about a friendly, cheerful atmosphere. If you wish, the hibachi can be placed on top of your regular gas or electric oven, or positioned in a fireplace if you have one. Always be sure you have satisfactory ventilation in the room, or the smoke created by the cooking may become a problem.

For hors d'oeuvre, small skewers suitable for cooking appetizer-sized kabobs are available. Also, miniature hibachis, just large enough to cook small amounts of food, are available in many specialty shops. These tiny hibachis are conversation pieces, and exceptionally useful for keeping foods hot.

PREPARING THE HIBACHI

1. Line the bottom of the hibachi with heavy-duty foil, to help keep it clean.
2. Allow twelve charcoal briquets for a regular-sized hibachi.
3. The grate should rest on the three metal projections located about an inch from the bottom.
4. Place the charcoal on the grate, sprinkle lightly with starter fluid, and ignite. In about ten minutes, the smoke will stop.
5. Put the grill atop the hibachi as soon as the flames die down to heat it. (For Genghis Khan cooking, put the wire mesh over the grill.)
6. Coals will be ready for cooking in about twenty minutes and will stay hot for about an hour. If a longer cooking time is required, add more charcoal after forty-five minutes or after the first flames die.
7. If the coals burn too fast, close the ventilator.

Chinese Barbecued Beef

2 pounds trimmed fillet of beef
½ cup soy sauce
1 tablespoon sugar
2 cloves garlic, minced
1 teaspoon salt
½ teaspoon freshly ground black pepper

Cut the beef into ¼-inch slices. Combine all remaining ingredients and marinate beef in mixture 2 hours, turning meat several times. Drain beef and place on a hibachi or larger grill about 4 inches above heat. Broil 2 minutes on each side.
Serves 6–8.

Genghis Khan Barbecue

Mongolian cooking from northern China is an ideal outdoor cooking method. Everyone cooks his/her food over a charcoal fire. For best results, the cooking unit should be placed in a position within everyone's reach. A hibachi is perfect for this type of cooking, but because the foods to be cooked are small, a piece of wire mesh should be placed over the grill to keep pieces from falling through. Provide each person with a small bowl of seasoning mix (recipe follows) into which the foods are dipped before cooking. Then, with chopsticks or fork, the meat or vegetables are held over the heat and grilled to the individual's taste. The food may also be cooked on a regular large grill, but it's more fun to have each person prepare his or her own.

SEASONING MIX

1½ cups soy sauce
1 cup water
3 cloves garlic, minced
3 tablespoons sugar

¾ cup thinly sliced green
onions
¾ cup minced parsley

Mix all the ingredients together, and divide among 6 to 8 bowls.

INGREDIENTS TO BE GRILLED

2 whole chicken breasts,
thinly sliced
1½ pounds thinly sliced
beef, pork, or lamb,
or a combination

Mushroom caps
Onion slices
Quartered green
peppers
Eggplant slices

Remove skin and bone from chicken breasts. Cut breasts in half and then, with sharp knife, cut each half breast into 3 fillets.

Arrange ingredients in individual groups and place on the table.

Serves 6–8.

Glazed Chicken and Beef, Japanese Style

SAUCE

½ cup sweet sake or dry
sherry
½ cup soy sauce
½ cup chicken broth

2 tablespoons sugar
4 teaspoons cornstarch
2 tablespoons cold water

Heat sake in a 1-quart saucepan; remove from heat and set aflame. When the flames die, add soy sauce, chicken broth, and sugar. Bring to a boil over low heat. Mix cornstarch with water and stir into the saucepan; cook, stirring constantly, until thickened and clear.

BEEF

1½ pounds fillet of beef

Slice fillet ¼ inch thick. Dip slices one by one into the sauce, coating both sides. Grill on a hibachi or grill about 1 minute on each side, or until brown.

CHICKEN

3 whole chicken breasts

Cut the breasts in half through the breastbone. Remove the skin and bones. Cut each breast in half, to make it thinner. Pound each piece lightly.

Dip slices into the sauce, one at a time, then cook on a hibachi or grill 2 inches over the heat, 2 to 3 minutes on each side.

Serves 6–8.

Mixed Grilled Meat, Korean Style

- 2 whole chicken breasts
- 2 pounds boneless pork, sliced thin
- 2 pounds fillet of beef, sliced thin
- ¾ cup sugar
- 1 cup soy sauce
- 2 tablespoons minced garlic
- 1 cup minced scallions
- ½ cup ground sesame seeds
- 1 tablespoon minced ginger root
- ½ teaspoon dried ground red pepper
- ¼ cup sesame-seed oil

Remove the chicken skin and bones. Cut each breast in half, then into paper-thin slices. Toss chicken, pork, and beef slices with sugar.

Mix all remaining ingredients. Dip chicken and meat slices in mixture, coating well. Let stand 1 hour.

Use a small grill or hibachi, and provide chopsticks or long forks for each guest to enable each to hold the meat over the heat and cook it to individual taste. The meats may also be cooked on a large grill, but only for a few minutes.

Serves 12–14.

Spiced Pork Chops, Korean Style

12 pork chops, ¼ inch thick	¼ teaspoon dried ground
½ cup soy sauce	red pepper
½ cup sake or dry sherry	2 teaspoons minced garlic
2 tablespoons vegetable oil	2 teaspoons minced ginger
½ teaspoon dry mustard	root

Rinse and dry the chops. Mix all remaining ingredients. Marinate chops in mixture for 2 hours, turning them several times to coat both sides. Drain, reserving marinade.

Arrange chops on a hibachi or larger grill, 3 inches over heat. Grill 20 minutes, or until no pink shows in center, basting and turning several times.

Serves 6–12.

Thai Shrimp Skewers

24 large raw shrimp,
   cleaned
1 cup pineapple juice
2 tablespoons lemon juice
2 tablespoons tomato
   paste

1½ teaspoons salt
¾ teaspoon freshly ground
   black pepper
18 canned lichee nuts

Wash and dry the shrimp. Mix pineapple juice, lemon juice, tomato paste, salt, and pepper. Marinate shrimp in mixture for 1 hour, then drain. Using 6 skewers, thread, alternating shrimp and lichees, starting and ending with the shrimp. Grill 4 inches over heat for 4 minutes on each side. Baste several times with marinade.

Serves 6.

10

Skewers and Kabobs

THE MIDDLE EAST is famous for its kabobs (which may also be spelled kebobs, kebabs, and so forth). It is pronounced and written somewhat differently all over the world, but its popularity is uniform everywhere. Wandering about the streets of the many cities and villages located at the eastern end of the Mediterranean, you'll see small open fires or grills, upon which kabobs are constantly being cooked and offered for sale to the people.

In Indonesia, Malaysia, and Singapore, they're called *sates*; however, they're still part of the family of skewers and kabobs. They can be prepared on small, moistened lengths of bamboo, although metal skewers may sometimes be employed. In Turkey and some other Middle East countries, it's a matter of pride for the host or hostess to use particularly beautiful metal skewers, often engraved with lovely designs.

The following recipes can be served as appetizers or, in some cases, as the main course of a meal.

Beef Brochette, Italian Style

8 thin slices steak, about 4 inches square	1 cup chopped onions
4 tablespoons olive oil	8 slices tomato
1 cup fresh breadcrumbs	1 teaspoon salt
⅓ cup grated Romano cheese	½ teaspoon freshly ground black pepper
3 tablespoons minced parsley	16 bay leaves

Pound the beef as thin as possible and dip each piece in oil. Mix breadcrumbs, cheese, and parsley. Spread some on each slice of beef, then cover with chopped onions and a slice of tomato. Sprinkle with salt and pepper. Roll up, and fasten with a skewer, with a bay leaf on each end.

Arrange the rolls on an oiled double-hinged wire grill. Grill 4 inches above heat 20 minutes, turning the grill to brown all sides.

Serves 4–8.

Beef Kabobs, Balinese Style

3 pounds boneless sirloin
    steak
½ teaspoon freshly ground
    black pepper
½ cup chopped chutney
½ cup ketchup
⅓ cup soy sauce

1 clove garlic, sliced
¼ cup lemon juice
2 tablespoons vegetable oil
1 large pineapple
2 green peppers
12 small white onions,
    peeled

Cut steak into 1-inch cubes. In a blender container, combine pepper, chutney, ketchup, soy sauce, garlic, lemon juice, and oil. Blend until smooth. Pour into a glass or pottery bowl and marinate meat in mixture overnight in the refrigerator, or for 2 hours at room temperature, turning occasionally. Drain, reserving marinade.

Peel the pineapple and cut into 1½-inch chunks. Cut green peppers into 1-inch cubes. Cut onions in half crosswise.

On each of 12 skewers, thread a steak cube, pineapple chunk, green pepper cube, and half of an onion; repeat, ending with a steak cube; brush with marinade and arrange on a rack 6 inches above heat. Grill 15 minutes, basting and turning skewers several times to brown all sides. Heat remaining marinade and serve as a sauce.

Serves 6–12.

Beef Skewers, Florentine Style

4 pounds boneless sirloin
    steak
1 cup olive oil
3 cups dry red wine
2½ teaspoons salt
1 teaspoon freshly ground
    black pepper

1 cup chopped fresh
    rosemary
Mushroom caps
Small white onions, half
    cooked
½ cup cognac

Cut the beef into 1½-inch cubes. Mix together oil, wine, salt, and pepper. Marinate meat in mixture for 2 hours. Drain. Roll the pieces lightly in rosemary.

Thread 10 to 12 skewers, alternating a piece of meat, a mushroom cap, and an onion, repeating until all the meat is used. Arrange the skewers on a grill 6 inches above heat. Grill 8 to 10 minutes, turning skewers frequently. Transfer skewers to a heated serving dish. Set the cognac aflame and pour over the skewers.

Serves 10–12.

Gaucho Beef Skewers, Argentine Style

4 pounds boneless sirloin steak
1½ cups dry white wine
½ cup wine vinegar
2 cups chopped onions
2 teaspoons oregano
Vegetable oil
¼ pound butter, melted
2 teaspoons salt
1 teaspoon freshly ground black pepper
¼ cup chopped parsley

Cut meat into 1½-inch cubes. Mix wine with wine vinegar, onions, and oregano. Marinate meat in mixture 5 hours at room temperature, or overnight in the refrigerator, turning occasionally. Drain, reserving marinade.

Thread meat on 10 to 12 skewers, leaving a bit of space between the cubes. Brush meat with oil. Arrange skewers 6 inches above heat and grill 8 to 10 minutes, turning the skewers frequently.

Meanwhile, combine butter, salt, pepper, parsley, and remaining marinade. Bring to a boil and cook over low heat 5 minutes. Serve as a sauce with the meat.

Serves 10–12.

Bulgarian Beef and Eggplant Skewers

3 pounds boneless sirloin
      steak, 1½ inches
      thick
1 2-pound eggplant
½ cup dry white wine

¼ cup lemon juice
2 cloves garlic, minced
   Pepper
   Cherry tomatoes
   Salt

Cut meat into 1½-inch cubes. Mix wine with wine and cut into 1-inch cubes. Mix wine, lemon juice, garlic, and pepper. Marinate beef and eggplant in mixture for ½ hour. Drain, reserving marinade. Thread alternately on 8 skewers the steak, eggplant, and cherry tomatoes; repeat several times, ending with steak.

Grill 4 inches above heat for 8 to 10 minutes, basting with marinade and turning skewers several times.

Serves 8.

Spiced Beef on Skewers, Indonesian Style

2 pounds sirloin steak, ½
      inch thick
2 teaspoons minced garlic
2 teaspoons ground
      caraway seeds
2 teaspoons ground
      coriander seeds

4 teaspoons brown sugar
3 tablespoons soy sauce
2 tablespoons lemon juice
1½ teaspoons salt
¼ teaspoon ground red
      pepper

Cut the meat into ½-inch cubes. Mix all remaining ingredients. Add meat, and toss well to coat the pieces. Let stand 1½ hours, turning meat several times.

Thread 5 pieces of meat on each of 30 small skewers (bamboo if available). Place 4 inches above heat, and grill 10 minutes, turning to brown all sides. Serve as hot hors d'oeuvre, and, if desired, use Saté Sauce as a dip (see page 173).

Yields about 30 skewers.

VARIATIONS

Chicken: Cut boned chicken breasts into ½-inch cubes. Proceed as directed.

Pork: Cut boneless pork into ½-inch cubes. Proceed as directed, but increase grilling time to 20 minutes.

Japanese Soy Chicken and Giblets

2 whole chicken breasts	½ cup chicken broth
½ pound chicken livers	2 tablespoons minced
½ pound chicken gizzards	ginger root
1 cup mirind (sweet sake)	3 tablespoons sugar
or medium sherry	Freshly ground pepper
1 cup soy sauce	Chopped parsley

Remove skin and bones from chicken breasts; cut into fairly uniform 1-inch slices. Wash livers and gizzards and cut each in half.

Mix all remaining ingredients in a saucepan. Bring to a boil and let cool. Pour into a bowl, and add the chicken pieces, livers, and gizzards. Let stand 1 hour. Drain, reserving the marinade.

Thread the ingredients alternately on 16 small skewers. Place on a grill 5 inches above heat and broil 10 minutes, turning skewers to brown all sides and basting with marinade. Serve with freshly ground black pepper and chopped fresh parsley.

Serves 4–8.

Chicken Kabobs, Middle East Style

3 whole chicken breasts
¼ cup yogurt
1 teaspoon salt
1 tablespoon curry powder
⅛ teaspoon dry mustard
½ teaspoon turmeric

1 tablespoon lemon juice
12 cherry tomatoes
12 pickled onions
Chopped fresh mint or
parsley

Remove the skin and bones from chicken breasts and cut them into thin 1-inch squares. Mix yogurt, seasonings, and lemon juice. Marinate chicken in mixture for 1 hour; drain.

Using 6 skewers, thread 1 piece of chicken, 1 tomato, 1 chicken piece, 1 onion, and repeat, ending with a piece of chicken. Grill 6 inches above heat for 10 minutes, turning skewers frequently to cook all sides. Serve sprinkled with mint or parsley.

Serves 6.

Curried Chicken Kabob, Singapore Style

4 whole chicken breasts
2 tablespoons curry powder
2 tablespoons chopped
chutney

½ cup dry white wine
¼ teaspoon Tabasco
1½ teaspoons salt
Vegetable oil

Remove skin and bones from chicken. Cut the meat into 1½-inch squares. Mix all remaining ingredients except the oil. Marinate chicken in mixture for 2 hours at room temperature or overnight in the refrigerator, turning occasionally.

Thread the chicken on 8 to 10 skewers. Brush with oil; arrange skewers 5 inches above heat. Grill 15 minutes, turning the skewers frequently.

Serves 8–10.

African Banana Skewers

4 bananas   Peanut butter
   Lemon juice

   Peel the bananas and cut into 1-inch slices. Sprinkle with
lemon juice and roll lightly in softened peanut butter. Thread
4 pieces of banana on each of 8 skewers. Broil 4 inches over
heat for 5 minutes, turning to brown all sides. Serve as hors
d'oeuvre.
   Serves 8.

Fruit Kabobs (Hawaiian)

1 16-ounce can pineapple   1 tablespoon honey
     chunks   1 clove garlic, minced
¼ cup dry red wine   3 canned yams
2 tablespoons lemon juice   3 very firm bananas
2 tablespoons vegetable oil   12 small white onions

   Drain pineapple; combine pineapple juice with wine,
lemon juice, oil, honey, and garlic.
   Cut the yams into 2-inch chunks and the bananas in 1-
inch-thick slices. Add yams, bananas, and onions to marinade.
Let stand in refrigerator overnight, or for at least 2 hours at
room temperature. Turn several times; drain, reserving marinade.
   Alternately thread pineapple, yam, banana, and an onion,
then repeat, ending with a cube of pineapple, on 12 skewers.
Grill 5 inches above heat 8 to 10 minutes, turning skewers
to brown all sides, brushing with marinade as you turn.
   Serves 12.

Middle East Kabobs

¼ cup dry red wine
¼ cup olive oil
2 tablespoons grated onion
1 teaspoon crushed
    coriander
1 teaspoon ground ginger
1 teaspoon turmeric
1 clove garlic, minced

1 tablespoon salt
2 pounds boneless lamb,
    cut in 1½-inch cubes
Sliced onions
Sliced tomatoes
Sliced green peppers
Mushroom caps
½ cup melted butter

Mix wine, oil, onion, coriander, ginger, turmeric, garlic, and salt in a large glass bowl. Marinate lamb in mixture for 2 hours. Thread repeatedly the meat, onions, tomatoes, green peppers, and mushroom caps on each of 8 skewers, starting and ending with meat. Place 5 inches above heat and grill 10 minutes, turning skewers frequently and basting with butter.
Serves 8.

Armenian Shish Kabob

1½ pounds boneless leg of
    lamb
1½ cups dry red wine
1⅓ cups dry sherry
¼ teaspoon thyme
½ teaspoon marjoram
½ teaspoon Tabasco
½ teaspoon salt

2 onions, thinly sliced
18 small white onions
18 mushroom caps
18 squares green pepper
18 cubes eggplant
½ cup canned mushroom
    sauce

Cut lamb in 1-inch cubes. In a glass or pottery bowl (do not use metal) or a jar, combine red wine, 1 cup sherry, thyme, marjoram, Tabasco, salt, and sliced onions. Add meat and marinate in the refrigerator for 24 hours, turning occasionally. Drain.

Thread 6 skewers with meat, white onions, mushrooms, green pepper, and eggplant; repeat several times. Mix remaining sherry with mushroom sauce and brush the skewered ingredients.

Place 5 inches above heat and grill 8 to 10 minutes, turning the skewers frequently. Serve with rice.

Serves 6.

Israeli Lamb Kabobs

2 pounds ground lamb (or beef)	2 teaspoons salt
¼ pound pine nuts or blanched almonds, chopped	½ teaspoon freshly ground black pepper
	¼ cup cold water
¾ cup minced onion	4 green peppers
½ cup chopped parsley	4 tomatoes
	Onion rings

Mix lamb (or if you prefer, beef), nuts, onion, parsley, salt, and pepper. Blend in water until the mixture holds together. Form 2-inch balls. Cut each pepper and tomato into 6 or 8 wedges.

Using 8 skewers, alternately place a lamb ball, tomato, lamb ball, and green pepper, until all are used. Place the skewers 5 inches over heat, and grill 10 minutes, turning the skewers frequently.

Serves 8.

Ground Lamb Kabobs, Indian Style

1½ pounds ground lamb
1 cup minced onion
2 cloves garlic, minced
1½ teaspoons salt
½ teaspoon freshly ground
    black pepper
1 teaspoon turmeric
1 teaspoon ground
    coriander seeds
½ teaspoon powdered
    ginger
½ cup yogurt

Mix all ingredients together until well blended. Form into 12 sausage shapes about 4 inches long.

Arrange on a greased double-hinged wire grill. Grill 5 inches above heat for 20 minutes, turning rack to brown all sides. Serve with a bowl of yogurt if desired.

Serves 6–8.

Lamb Skewers, Greek Style

3 pounds boneless lamb
½ cup olive oil
1 cup dry red wine
2 teaspoons salt
½ teaspoon freshly ground
    black pepper
1 teaspoon crumbled
    oregano
⅓ teaspoon crumbled dried
    mint
1 clove garlic, minced

This dish is best made with leg of lamb. Cut the meat into 1-inch cubes. Thread the cubes on 8 to 12 skewers.

In a long shallow pan, mix all remaining ingredients. Place the skewered meat in marinade; let stand 2 hours. Baste frequently.

Arrange the skewers 4 inches above heat and grill 10 minutes, turning and basting frequently.

Serves 8–12.

Lamb on Skewers, Moroccan Style

2 pounds leg of lamb	3 tomatoes
¼ cup lemon juice	1 large onion, peeled and
2 tablespoons olive oil	sliced
2 teaspoons salt	1 eggplant (optional)
½ teaspoon freshly ground	1 green pepper (optional)
black pepper	Bay leaves

Cut meat into 1-inch cubes. Mix lemon juice and olive oil in a bowl. Add lamb and toss until all pieces are coated; season with salt and pepper. Cut each tomato into 6 wedges. Place tomatoes and onion over the lamb and let stand for 4 hours.

If you're using the optional eggplant, peel and cut into ½-inch slices, then into 1-inch squares. Cut the optional green pepper into 1-inch squares.

Thread 8 skewers, alternating 1 cube of lamb, 1 wedge of tomato, 1 eggplant square, 1 green pepper square, and 1 bay leaf. Repeat several times.

Place on grill about 4 inches above heat and grill 15 minutes, turning the skewers several times.

Serves 8.

Russian Shashlik

3 pounds rump of lamb	1 large onion, sliced
2 teaspoons salt	½ cup chopped parsley
¾ teaspoon freshly ground	1 cup cider vinegar
black pepper	1 cup water
2 cloves garlic, sliced	⅛ teaspoon allspice

Cut the meat into 2½-inch cubes. Place in a glass or pottery bowl and season with salt and pepper. Cover meat with garlic, onion, and parsley.

Combine vinegar, water, and allspice and bring to a boil. Cook 2 minutes, then cool. Pour over meat. Cover bowl and let marinate in the refrigerator overnight. Turn the meat several times.

When ready to cook, drain and dry the meat. Thread the meat on 8 skewers. Place on grill 5 inches above heat, with a drip pan underneath. Grill 15 minutes, turning the skewers frequently to brown all sides. Baste with any drippings. Serve with lemon quarters.

Serves 8.

Satay Singapura

MEAT AND MARINADE

3 pounds boneless lamb or beef

½ cup peanut or vegetable oil

¼ cup sugar

¼ teaspoon powdered saffron

1 tablespoon ground coriander seeds

2 teaspoons salt

2 tablespoons grated lemon rind

Cut meat into 1-inch cubes. Mix remaining ingredients and marinate meat in mixture. Refrigerate for 24 hours, basting and turning occasionally.

SAUCE

2 tablespoons peanut or
    vegetable oil
½ cup minced onion
⅛ teaspoon Tabasco
1½ cups peanut butter

1 cup plum jam
½ cup lemon juice
2 cups water
2 tablespoons sugar
1 teaspoon salt

Heat oil in a saucepan; sauté onions 10 minutes, stirring frequently. Mix Tabasco, peanut butter, plum jam, lemon juice, and water until smooth. Add to onions and cook for 15 minutes, stirring frequently. Stir in sugar and salt, then cook an additional 10 minutes.

Thread meat on 12 to 16 skewers. Place 5 inches above heat and grill 8 to 10 minutes, turning to brown all sides.

Pour hot sauce into a gravy boat. You may dip the satay in the sauce or spoon it over the meat.

Serves 6–12.

Turkish Lamb and Vegetable Kabobs

2 pounds boneless lamb
4 teaspoons salt
2 large potatoes
3 green peppers

16 mushroom caps
16 small white onions
16 cherry tomatoes
    Vegetable oil

Cut the meat into 1½-inch cubes. Sprinkle with half the salt. Cook the potatoes in boiling water for 10 minutes. Drain, cool, peel, and cut potatoes into 1-inch slices. Cut the green peppers into squares.

Thread 8 skewers, alternating the meat and vegetables. Repeat, ending with meat. Sprinkle with remaining salt and brush with oil. Grill 5 inches above heat for 12 to 15 minutes, turning the skewers to brown all sides.

Serves 8.

Chicken Livers on Skewers, Chilean Style

18 chicken livers
6 slices bacon
12 button mushroom caps
  Melted butter
  Salt
  Freshly ground black
    pepper
½ cup sifted cracker meal

Wash livers, removing any discolored areas; cut each in half. Cut bacon in 1-inch pieces. On each of 6 skewers, thread a mushroom cap, then squares of livers and bacon, repeating until ingredients are all threaded, with mushrooms on each end. Brush with melted butter. Sprinkle with salt and pepper and roll in the cracker meal on wax paper.

Arrange on a small grill (or hibachi) 3 inches above heat and grill 10 minutes, turning skewers frequently and brushing with melted butter.

Serves 6.

Liver with Apples, German Style

1 pound calf's liver, cut
  into ½-inch-thick
  slices
10 small white onions, half
  cooked and drained
2 cooking apples, peeled
  and cut into ½-inch
  cubes
1 teaspoon salt
½ teaspoon freshly ground
  black pepper
½ cup melted butter

Cut 4-inch cubes of liver. Rinse and dry. Thread 12 small skewers, alternating the liver, onions, and apple cubes. Sprinkle with salt and pepper and brush with melted butter.

Grill 4 inches above heat for 10 minutes, turning and basting with butter several times.

Serves 4–6.

Liver Kabobs, Indian Style

2 pounds calf's liver	2 tablespoons chili powder
¾ cup lemon juice	4 tablespoons melted
2 teaspoons salt	butter

Wash and dry the liver. Cut into 1-inch-square pieces.

Mix lemon juice, salt, and half of the chili powder. Marinate liver in mixture for 30 minutes; drain.

Thread liver on 8 or 10 skewers. Sprinkle with remaining chili powder. Place 4 inches over heat and cook 10 minutes, turning and brushing with melted butter several times.

Serves 8–10.

Indonesian Steak Satay

½ cup packaged fine-grated coconut	½ teaspoon ground coriander
¾ cup heavy cream	½ teaspoon turmeric
2 pounds sirloin steak, ½ inch thick	1 teaspoon sugar
½ cup minced onions	¾ cup ground almonds
1 clove garlic, minced	3 tablespoons sesame or vegetable oil
1½ teaspoons salt	2 tablespoons lemon juice
½ teaspoon Tabasco	

Rinse the coconut under cold running water; drain and combine with cream in a saucepan; bring to a boil. Let stand 30 minutes, drain well and discard coconut; reserve the cream.

Cut the steak in ¾-inch squares. Chop or pound the onions, garlic, salt, Tabasco, coriander, turmeric, sugar, and almonds to a paste. Toss the meat with the mixture and let stand 2 hours. Thread the meat onto 8 skewers. Reserve any of the spice mixture that doesn't adhere. Grill 3 inches above heat 8 minutes, or to desired degree of rareness, turning skewers frequently.

While the meat is grilling, combine coconut cream, oil, lemon juice, and the reserved spice in a saucepan. Bring to a boil and cook 5 minutes over low heat and serve as sauce with the broiled meat.

Serves 8.

Australian Sausage Skewers

6 bratwurst or 12 pork
    sausages
2 tablespoons prepared
    mustard

18 pickled onions

Cook bratwurst or sausages in boiling water for 5 minutes; drain and cool. Cut each bratwurst in 4 pieces crosswise (or each sausage in half crosswise). Brush lightly with mustard. Thread the bratwurst (or sausages) alternately with the onions on 6 skewers, starting and ending with the meat. Grill 4 inches above heat for 10 minutes, turning the skewers frequently to brown all sides.

Serves 6.

Japanese Meat Skewers

1½ pounds boneless beef or
    pork, 1 inch thick
2 green peppers
24 mushrooms
8 green onions
⅓ cup soy sauce

¼ cup sake or beer
1 tablespoon sugar
½ teaspoon ground ginger
¼ teaspoon monosodium
    glutamate
Dash cayenne pepper

Cut meat into 1½-inch squares. Wash peppers, remove seeds, and cut into 1-inch squares. Rinse and dry mushrooms. Wash, clean, and cut green onions into 2-inch lengths. Thread 6 to 8 bamboo skewers, alternating the meat and vegetables.

Combine all remaining ingredients in a large glass or pottery bowl or dish. Marinate skewered ingredients in mixture for 1 hour, turning occasionally. Drain, reserving marinade.

Place the skewers on the grill about 3 inches above heat. Grill beef 10 minutes, pork 15 (or until no pink shows in center), turning the skewers and basting with marinade several times.

Serves 6–8.

Kidneys on Skewers, Italian Style

4 veal kidneys	½ cup grated onion
8 strips bacon, quartered crosswise	2 teaspoons salt
¾ cup dry red wine	½ teaspoon freshly ground black pepper
⅓ cup vegetable oil	½ teaspoon dry mustard

Wash the kidneys and cut into 1-inch cubes, discarding membranes. Soak in salted ice water for 30 minutes; drain.

Mix wine, oil, onion, salt, pepper, and mustard. Add kidneys and marinate in the refrigerator for 2 hours, basting several times. Drain, reserving marinade.

Thread 8 skewers, alternating the kidneys and bacon. Arrange on a grill 5 inches above heat. Grill 15 minutes, basting and turning several times.

Serves 4–8.

Peruvian Skewered Barbecued Meat

1 beef heart (2 pounds), or
  2 pounds sirloin
  steak
1½ teaspoons salt
½ teaspoon dried ground
  red peppers

6 peppercorns, crushed
½ teaspoon saffron
3 cloves garlic, minced
1 cup wine vinegar
½ cup water
½ cup olive oil

Beef heart is used in Peru when preparing *anticuchos,* but steak is a tasty substitute. Wash the heart, remove skin, and cut into 1-inch cubes (or cut 1-inch cubes of steak). Mix in a bowl salt, red peppers, peppercorns, saffron, garlic, vinegar, and water. Marinate meat in mixture overnight in the refrigerator, turning occasionally.

Drain meat, reserving marinade. Thread the meat on 4 to 6 skewers; brush with olive oil. Grill 4 inches above heat for 10 minutes or until heart is tender (or steak reaches desired degree of rareness). Turn skewers and baste frequently with marinade.

Serves 4–6.

Polynesian Ham Skewers

2 pounds ham steak, 1
  inch thick
Pineapple wedges

Bananas, cut in 2-inch
  slices
Orange-flavored liqueur

Cut 1-inch cubes of ham. Thread 6 skewers, alternating the ham cubes, pineapple wedges, and bananas, starting and ending with ham. Grill 6 inches above heat, brushing with orange liqueur once or twice and turning the skewers frequently.

Serves 6.

Pork Brochettes, French Style

3 pork tenderloins (fillets),
    about 2½ pounds
½ cup vegetable oil
¼ cup brandy
½ cup minced onion

2 cloves garlic, minced
1½ teaspoons salt
½ teaspoon freshly ground
    black pepper

Wash and dry the pork and cut each fillet into slices about 1 inch thick. Mix all remaining ingredients. Marinate pork in mixture for at least 2 hours, or overnight in the refrigerator if possible. Turn and baste meat several times. Drain meat and divide among 8 skewers. Reserve marinade. Grill 6 inches above heat for 25 minutes with a drip pan underneath, turning and basting with marinade several times.

Serves 8.

Yugoslavian Mixed Barbecue

1½ pounds boneless leg of
    pork
1½ pounds sirloin steak, 1½
    inches thick
1 pound onions, peeled
    and sliced
3 teaspoons salt
1 teaspoon freshly ground
    black pepper

1 teaspoon paprika
½ cup fresh or frozen
    blueberries, crushed
½ cup dry white wine
Cherry tomatoes
Pickled onions
¼ pound bacon, cut into
    ½-inch cubes

Cut both pork and steak into 1½-inch cubes.

Place one layer of onions and one layer of meat in a deep dish. Season with salt, pepper, and paprika. Spread a portion of the blueberries over, and add some wine. Repeat the layers. Cover the dish and refrigerate for 4 hours. Drain.

Thread a piece of pork, a tomato, a piece of beef, a pickled onion, and a slice of bacon on each of 8 skewers. Repeat several times, ending with a piece of meat. Grill 5 inches above heat for 20 minutes, turning skewers frequently.

Serves 8.

Grilled Clams, Japanese Style

½ cup soy sauce
½ cup sake or dry sherry
2 tablespoons vegetable oil

4 tablespoons condensed
   black bean soup
36 shucked clams

Mix soy sauce, wine, oil, and black bean soup in a saucepan. Bring to a boil.

Thread 4 to 6 clams on small skewers. Dip in soy mixture in shallow bowl. Grill 5 inches over heat for about 5 minutes, turning the skewers to cook all sides. Serve reheated sauce with clams.

Serves 6–8.

Oyster Brochettes, English Style

36 shucked oysters
   Freshly ground black
      pepper

18 slices bacon

Dry the oysters; sprinkle with pepper. Cut bacon slices in half, crosswise. Wrap a half slice around each oyster.

Thread 6 oysters on each of 6 skewers. Broil 4 inches over heat, until bacon is browned. Turn skewers frequently to brown all sides.

Serves 6.

Oysters, Louisiana Style

24 freshly shucked oysters	12 slices bacon
Freshly ground black pepper	18 frozen artichoke hearts, thawed

Dry the oysters and sprinkle with pepper. Cut each piece of bacon in half, crosswise, and wrap one piece around each oyster. Thread the oysters and artichoke hearts on each of 6 skewers, starting and ending with oysters. Grill 4 inches above heat for 5 minutes, turning skewers several times.

Serves 6.

Grilled Scallops, Japanese Style

1½ pounds scallops	2 teaspoons minced ginger root
1 cup soy sauce	
3 tablespoons sugar	

If bay scallops are used, leave them whole. Cut sea scallops in half.

In a saucepan, heat remaining ingredients to boiling, then reduce to simmer. Add scallops, cook 2 minutes. Let stand until cool enough to handle. Thread 4 to 6 scallops on small skewers. Grill 5 inches over heat for 4 minutes, turning to brown all sides.

Serves 10–12 as hors d'oeuvre.

Seafood Skewers, Chilean Style

36 raw shrimp
36 bay scallops or 18 sea
   scallops
1 cup dry vermouth
½ cup olive or vegetable
   oil

1½ teaspoons salt
1 clove garlic, minced
½ teaspoon Tabasco

Shell, devein, wash, and dry the shrimp. Wash and dry the scallops. Cut sea scallops in half.

Mix remaining ingredients; add seafood and mix thoroughly. Cover and marinate in refrigerator 3 hours. Drain, reserving marinade.

Thread on 12 skewers, alternating 3 shrimp and 3 scallops per skewer. Place the skewers on a rack 4 inches over heat. Grill 6 minutes, basting with marinade several times and turning skewers to cook all sides.

Serves 6–12.

Glazed Shrimp, Indonesian Style

2 pounds raw shrimp
¼ cup soy sauce
¼ cup lemon juice
3 tablespoons plum jam

¼ teaspoon ground red
   pepper
½ cup minced onions
1½ teaspoons salt

Shell shrimp, remove black vein; wash and dry.

Mix all remaining ingredients. Marinate shrimp in mixture for 1 hour.

The shrimp may be grilled on small skewers or individually on a greased close-mesh, double-hinged wire grill. Grill

5 inches above heat for 8 to 10 minutes, turning and basting several times. Serve on skewers, or pierce the individual shrimp with cocktail picks to serve as hors d'oeuvre.

Yields about 40.

Marinated Shrimp Kabobs, Indian Style

2 pounds raw shrimp, shelled and deveined
½ cup yogurt
½ cup vegetable oil
½ teaspoon freshly ground black pepper
½ teaspoon thyme
Salt

Wash and dry the shrimp. Mix together yogurt, oil, pepper, and thyme. Add shrimp and mix well to coat. Cover and let stand in refrigerator for 3 hours. Drain, reserving marinade.

Thread shrimp on 12 skewers and place 4 inches over heat. Grill 6 to 8 minutes, turning and basting with marinade several times. Sprinkle with salt.

Serves 6–12.

Grilled Shrimp, Tahitian Style

2 pounds raw shrimp
4 teaspoons cornstarch
1 cup pineapple juice
3 tablespoons honey
½ cup soy sauce
2 tablespoons cider vinegar
1 teaspoon powdered ginger

Remove shrimp shells, leaving the tails intact. Slit the backs and rinse under cold water to remove black vein. Dry. In a small saucepan, blend the cornstarch with a little of the pineapple juice until smooth, then stir in pineapple juice, honey, soy sauce, vinegar, and ginger. Bring to a boil, stirring constantly, then cook over low heat for 5 minutes. Cool.

Thread 4 to 6 shrimp on skewers, then dip in sauce, coating well. Grill 5 inches above heat for 6 minutes, turning the skewers to brown all sides. Reheat remaining sauce and serve with shrimp.

Serves 6–8.

Malaysian Barbecued Shrimp

24 large raw shrimp
8 chicken livers
8 slices bacon
½ cup soy sauce
4 teaspoons sugar
1 tablespoon minced

ginger root or
preserved ginger
1 clove garlic, minced
¼ teaspoon freshly ground
black pepper

Remove shrimp shells, but leave the tails intact. Slit shrimp, remove veins; wash and dry. Press each shrimp open.

Wash and dry the livers. Cut each liver in half. Cut each piece of bacon in half, crosswise, and wrap a piece of bacon around each piece of liver.

Mix soy sauce, sugar, ginger, garlic, and pepper. Marinate shrimp in mixture for 30 minutes, turning several times; drain.

Thread shrimp and bacon-wrapped livers on 6 or 8 skewers, starting and ending with shrimp. Place on grill about 5 inches over heat and broil 6 minutes, turning skewers several times to cook all sides.

Serves 6–8.

Orange Shrimp, Tahitian Style

2 pounds large raw shrimp	½ teaspoon ground ginger
⅓ cup soy sauce	2 cloves garlic, minced
⅓ cup orange juice	¼ cup vegetable oil
2 tablespoons dry sherry	4 navel oranges
1 teaspoon salt	

Remove the shrimp from shells, but leave the tails intact. Slit the backs and run under cold water to remove black vein; dry.

Combine in a bowl the soy sauce, orange juice, sherry, salt, ginger, garlic, and oil. Marinate shrimp in mixture for 4 hours in the refrigerator. Drain, reserving marinade.

Peel the oranges and cut each into 6 wedges. Alternately thread shrimp and orange wedges on 12 skewers. Arrange on a rack 6 inches above heat. Grill 10 minutes, brushing with marinade and turning skewers to cook all sides. Heat remaining marinade and serve as a sauce.

Serves 6–12.

Taiwan Shrimp

36 large shrimp	Dash ground ginger
¼ cup dry sherry	1 large pineapple, or 1
1½ teaspoons salt	large can pineapple
⅛ teaspoon freshly ground	chunks
black pepper	4 tablespoons melted
Dash cinnamon	butter

Shell and devein shrimp, then wash and dry. Mix sherry, salt, pepper, cinnamon, and ginger in a glass or pottery bowl. Add shrimp, turning to coat all sides. Marinate in the refrigerator for 2 hours, turning occasionally.

If a fresh pineapple is used, peel and cut into 30 cubes. If canned pineapple is used, drain well. Drain shrimp and, on 6 skewers, thread shrimp and pineapple on each, starting and ending with shrimp. Brush with melted butter. Place on grill about 5 inches above heat. Broil 8 to 10 minutes, basting frequently with melted butter. Turn skewers occasionally, to cook all sides.

Serves 6.

Swordfish and Melon Skewers, Mexican Style

2 pounds swordfish, ¾ inch thick
¾ cup lime or lemon juice

¼ cup chopped scallions
1½ teaspoons salt
1 large cantalope

Wash and dry the fish; cut into ¾-inch cubes. Mix lime juice, scallions, and salt. Marinate fish in mixture 1½ hours, basting several times.

Peel melon, discard seeds, and cut into ½-inch cubes. Drain the fish. Use about 30 long, thin wooden skewers and thread, alternating the fish and melon. Arrange on a regular grill (or hibachi), 2 inches over heat. Cook 5 to 6 minutes, turning several times to cook all sides.

Yields about 30.

Turkish Swordfish on Skewers

3 pounds swordfish or other firm-fleshed fish, 1 inch thick
¼ cup olive oil
¼ cup lemon juice
¼ cup grated onion

2 teaspoons salt
½ teaspoon freshly ground black pepper
Bay leaves
Lemon slices

Wash and dry the fish. Carefully remove the skin and cut fish into 1½-inch squares. Mix oil, lemon juice, onion, salt, and pepper. Marinate fish in mixture in the refrigerator overnight, or for at least 4 hours at room temperature. Baste and turn several times; drain.

Using 6 to 8 skewers, alternately thread squares of fish, 1 bay leaf, and 1 lemon slice, repeating several times, ending with a square of fish. Arrange on the grill about 5 inches above heat. Grill 10 to 12 minutes, turning skewers frequently and basting with marinade.

Serves 6–8.

11

Smoke Cookery

YOU MAY START the food preparation to be smoked two—
or even three—days before you want to serve it.

For smoking, a covered barbecue with a high dome or
tight-fitting lid is necessary. You'll need about twenty long-
burning charcoal briquets and about a pound and a half of
hickory or hardwood chips. Soak four cups of chips in a bowl
of cold water for fifteen to twenty minutes.

On the lower rack of the barbecue, make a mound of
twelve briquets and set afire. When coals look ashy-gray,

carefully move four to each far side of the rack. Put the remaining four hot coals in a small metal pan. Add four unlighted briquets to the four hot coals to ignite them. Put an aluminum-foil pan in the center of the barbecue to catch drippings.

Rub the top rack with oil. Center the food to be smoked so no part extends over the hot coals. (If you're using a thermometer, put it on top of or beside the meat, near the center of the grill.)

Drain two cups of chips and sprinkle them over the hot coals. Open the barbecue vents and close the lid. Check the temperature after ten minutes; the thermometer should register 140° F. to 145° F. If below that, add one hot coal to one side. If above, remove one.

Check the temperature every half hour, and add more hot coals to maintain the temperature. When smoke stops coming out of the vents, add more presoaked chips to the burning coals.

Smoking Pork Roasts

A 6-pound tied pork loin is a good size to buy. The meat need not be preseasoned, but for a more intense flavor, marinate it for 2 hours in one of the basic wine marinades. Dry thoroughly before placing in the smoke oven. Smoke meat for 3 hours.

The meat may be cooled, covered, and refrigerated for several days (it can also be frozen). If you plan to freeze it, thaw before completing the cooking process.

To complete the cooking, place roast in a shallow roasting pan and roast in a 350° F. oven for 2 hours (170° F. on a meat thermometer). Let stand 15 minutes before carving. Smoked pork is also good chilled and cut in thin slices.

Serves 8–12.

Smoked Brisket of Beef

1 6-pound corned or fresh brisket of beef	2 bay leaves
Water	2 cloves
6 cloves garlic, peeled and sliced	2 peppercorns

Rinse beef and place in large saucepan. Add water to cover, then garlic, bay leaves, cloves, and peppercorns (if fresh brisket is used, add 3 teaspoons salt as well). Bring to a boil, cover, and cook over low heat for 2½ hours or until tender. Drain, reserving water. Dry the meat and smoke as directed for 2 hours or until fat is golden brown.

Return meat to cooking water; bring to a boil, remove from heat, and let stand for 15 minutes. Drain and serve immediately (or for future use, cool, cover, and refrigerate or freeze until needed).

Serves 12–16.

Smoked Chicken

1 5-pound roasting chicken	2 cloves garlic, minced (optional)
2 teaspoons salt	
¾ teaspoon freshly ground black pepper	

Wash and dry the chicken; tie wings to body. Rub with mixture of salt, pepper, and garlic. Smoke as directed for 2½ hours. If you want to complete the cooking much faster, after smoking you may cook chicken in a roasting pan, and roast in a 350° F. oven for 45 minutes.

For future use, cool the smoked chicken, wrap, and

refrigerate (or freeze) until needed. If frozen, thaw before roasting; then roast 60 minutes.

To serve, cut thin slices.

Serves 6–8.

Smoked Duck

1 5-pound duck	½ teaspoon paprika
2 teaspoons salt	2 teaspoons minced garlic
¾ teaspoon freshly ground black pepper	

Wash and dry the duck and rub inside and out with a mixture of salt, pepper, paprika, and garlic. Smoke as directed for 2½ hours. Place in a shallow roasting pan and roast in a 400° F. oven for 45 minutes. Serve hot, in sections; or cold, sliced very thin.

Serves 6–8.

Smoked Pork Chops, Chinese Style

8 rib pork chops, 1 inch thick	1 teaspoon salt
½ cup soy sauce	¾ teaspoon freshly ground black pepper
3 tablespoons honey	2 teaspoons minced ginger root
2 cloves garlic, minced	

Rinse and dry the pork chops. Mix all remaining ingredients and brush the mixture over both sides of the chops. Let stand 1 hour.

Arrange chops on greased grill of smoke oven. Place a pan of water mixed with the marinade on the bottom. Cover and smoke 1 hour.

Serves 8.

Smoked Fish, Burmese Style

6 slices fish, 1 inch thick	2 tablespoons minced ginger root
2 teaspoons salt	
¼ teaspoon crumbled saffron	1 tablespoon tomato sauce
	2 tablespoons cider vinegar
3 tablespoons peanut oil	
2 cups thinly sliced onions	½ teaspoon dried ground red pepper
3 cloves garlic, minced	

Wash and dry the fish. Season with salt and saffron. Arrange fish in a greased heatproof baking dish.

Heat oil in a skillet; sauté onions 10 minutes. Stir in all remaining ingredients. Pour evenly over fish. Place dish on rack of the smoke oven. Place a pan of water in the bottom of the grill. Cover and smoke 1 hour. Serve hot or cold.

Serves 6.

Smoked Salmon, Finnish Style

1 6-pound half salmon (halved lengthwise)	2 teaspoons crushed white peppercorns
2 teaspoons coarse (Kosher) salt	12 sprigs dill

Bone the salmon. Wash and dry. Press salt and pepper-corns into the cut side of the salmon, and spread the dill over it. Place in grill, skin side down. Smoke as directed 1½ hours. Chill and cut thin slices.

Serves 24 as appetizer.

Smoked Trout, Danish Style

6 whole trout
3 teaspoons salt

1 teaspoon freshly ground
   white pepper

Wash and dry the trout. Rub with salt and pepper. Arrange on grill of smoke oven. Smoke as directed for 1 hour. Serve with a mixture of 1 cup sour cream and ¼ cup horseradish.

Serves 6–12.

Smoked Spareribs, Chinese Style

2 racks spareribs
½ cup soy sauce
3 tablespoons honey
2 tablespoons sugar

1 teaspoon salt
¾ teaspoon freshly ground
   black pepper

Crack the spareribs crosswise through the middle. Wash and dry. Mix together all remaining ingredients; coat both sides of the spareribs. Let stand 2 hours, basting frequently. Drain.

Place the ribs on the lower rack of the smoke oven. Put marinade in a pan and add 2 cups water. Place in bottom of grill; cover and smoke 2½ hours. To serve, cut into individual ribs.

Serves 4–6.

Smoked Turkey

1 15-pound turkey	¼ cup melted butter
1 tablespoon salt	
1 teaspoon freshly ground black pepper	

Wash and ary the turkey. Rub inside and out with salt and pepper; tie wings to body. Smoke as directed 4 hours. Transfer turkey to a shallow roasting pan and roast in a 375° F. oven for 2 hours, basting frequently with melted butter. Serve hot or cold. If you wish, the turkey can be frozen or refrigerated for future use. If so, cool after cooking, then wrap and refrigerate (only for up to 2 days), or freeze until needed.

Serves 12–16.

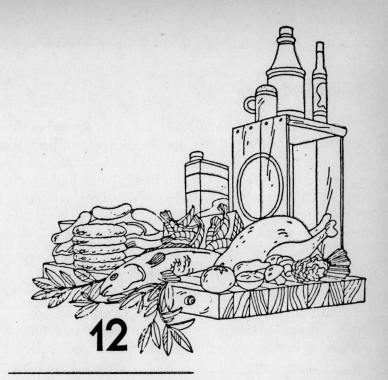

12

Vegetables

OF COURSE, the primary purpose of using a grill is for barbecuing meats, poultry, and fish. However, while cooking in this fashion, it's often a good idea to prepare a vegetable at the same time, using the corners or edges not in use. (Also included is a bread recipe.) These recipes are particularly suited to grill cookery and have been prepared to provide unusual and interesting flavors. Of course, the recipes that follow are merely suggestions, and you can prepare others using whatever happens to be in season at the time by following these methods.

Barbecued Corn

Remove the corn from husks and silk. Spread each ear with softened butter. Cut a double thickness of heavy-duty aluminum foil large enough to enfold each ear of corn. Place an ear on each piece (or, if you like, 2 ears), fold over, and seal firmly. Place grill 6 inches above heat, and cook 20 minutes (or until corn is tender), turning the packets several times with tongs. Unfold packages and sprinkle with salt.

Parmesan Cheese Bread, Italian Style

1 loaf Italian bread, about 18 inches long	½ cup freshly grated Parmesan cheese
¼ pound butter, at room temperature	¼ cup chopped parsley, Italian if available

Make vertical cuts in bread about every 1½ inches (but don't cut down to the bottom crust).

Blend all remaining ingredients and spread mixture heavily in the cuts. Wrap loaf in heavy-duty aluminum foil and place it on a rack 6 inches above heat. Grill 15 minutes, turning the loaf several times. Unwrap and cut through the bottom crust.

Serves 8–12.

Stuffed Eggplant, Burmese Style

2 2-pound eggplants	1½ teaspoons salt
¼ pound (1 stick) butter	¾ teaspoon pepper
2 cups chopped onions	2 teaspoons turmeric
1 pound ground beef	2 cups yogurt
2 teaspoons ground cumin seeds	

Wash and dry the eggplants. Cut a 2-inch piece off the stem end and reserve. Scoop out and chop eggplant pulp.

Melt butter in a skillet; pour off about 2 tablespoons and set aside. Add onions to the remaining butter and sauté 5 minutes. Then add the chopped eggplant, beef, cumin, salt, and pepper. Sauté an additional 10 minutes, stirring frequently. Cool, then stuff the eggplants. Replace the tops, and fasten with small skewers or toothpicks.

Cut 2 pieces of heavy-duty aluminum foil large enough to enfold the eggplants. Mix remaining butter with turmeric and yogurt. Spread some on each piece of foil, and place an eggplant over it. Cover with remaining yogurt. Fold up the foil, securely sealing the edges. Place on a grill 5 inches above heat and grill 45 minutes, turning the packages several times. Unfold packages and slice crosswise.

Serves 4–8.

Barbecued Potatoes

Use medium-sized baking potatoes. Wash, scrub, and dry. Brush each with oil and wrap each potato (or two, if you prefer) in a piece of heavy-duty foil. Arrange on the back of the grill, and bake 50 minutes (or until tender). Turn potatoes several times. Unwrap, slash tops, and put a pat of butter in each.

Stuffed Squash, German Style

4 medium-sized acron squash	1 cup packed brown sugar
3 tablespoons melted butter	½ cup coarsely chopped walnuts
1 teaspoon salt	¼ teaspoon nutmeg
1 pound green apples, cut in ½-inch cubes	

Cut squash in half lengthwise, and scoop out seeds and fibers. Brush cut sides and edges with melted butter and sprinkle with salt.

Place, cut side down, on a rack 5 inches above heat and grill 30 minutes. Then turn skin side down.

Mix apples, brown sugar, nuts, and nutmeg. Fill squash cavities with mixture and grill an additional 30 minutes.

Serves 8.

Micronesian Skewered Sweet Potatoes and Oranges

4 large sweet potatoes
16 slices bacon

4 oranges
½ cup sugar

Cook sweet potatoes in salted boiling water to cover for 20 minutes. Drain, and peel when cool enough to handle. Cut each in quarters and wrap each in a piece of bacon. Peel and quarter the oranges; dip each quarter in sugar. Thread 6 skewers with the potatoes and oranges, being sure the open end of the bacon is secured. Broil 4 inches above heat for 10 minutes, turning frequently.

Serves 6.

Sweet Potatoes, Fijian Style

6 sweet potatoes
4 tablespoons butter
2 teaspoons salt
4 tablespoons orange juice
1 cup crushed canned
    pineapple, drained

1 tablespoon grated orange
    rind
2 bananas, sliced
6 teaspoons brown sugar

Wash and dry the potatoes. Bake in a 375°F. oven 45 minutes (or until tender). Cut in half lengthwise and scoop out pulp, leaving about a ¼-inch shell. Mash potato pulp with butter and salt, then beat in orange juice, pineapple, and orange rind until fluffy.

Line potato shells with slices of banana, and heap on sweet potato mixture. Sprinkle with brown sugar.

Cut 12 pieces of heavy-duty aluminum foil large enough to enclose the potatoes. Place a filled potato half on each; fold up foil, and seal edges securely.

Place on the sides of the grill, 5 inches above heat. Cook 30 minutes. To serve, fold back the foil.

Serves 12.

Stuffed Tomatoes, Polish Style

4 large firm tomatoes	⅓ cup dry breadcrumbs
Salt	1 teaspoon crushed basil
¼ cup butter, softened	¼ cup minced parsley
½ cup grated mozzarella or Muenster cheese	Vegetable oil

Wash and dry the tomatoes, then cut in half crosswise. Scoop out pulp with a small spoon and sprinkle the shells with salt. Chop the pulp. Beat butter with cheese, then mix in pulp, breadcrumbs, basil, and parsley. Firmly stuff the shells with mixture.

Cut 8 pieces of heavy-duty aluminum foil large enough to completely enclose a tomato half. Grease the foil with oil and place a tomato half on each. Fold up foil, sealing edges. Place on grill, stuffed side up, 5 inches above heat. Grill 15 to 20 minutes. Fold back the foil to serve.

Serves 8.

Grilled Zucchini, Italian Style

2 pounds small zucchini	½ cup vegetable oil
Water	2 cloves garlic, minced
2 teaspoons salt	½ teaspoon crushed basil

Use only very small zucchini. Scrub with a brush under cold running water, then cut off the ends. Place in a saucepan and add salt and water to cover. Bring to a boil and cook 10 minutes. Drain very well and dry.

Mix all remaining ingredients in a long, glass baking dish and marinate zucchini in the mixture 1 hour. Drain, reserving marinade.

Arrange the zucchini on a grill 5 inches above heat. Grill 15 minutes, basting and turning several times.

Serves 4–6.

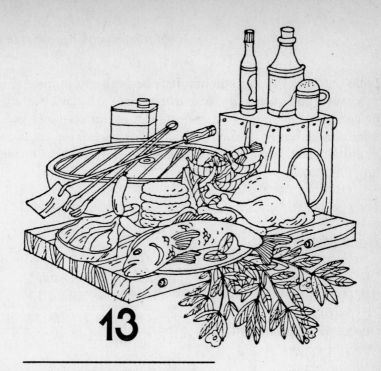

13

Marinades and Sauces

THIS SECTION CONTAINS RECIPES for basic marinades and sauces, ideally suited for the particular foods suggested. These marinades and sauces are convenient for impromptu use, when you wish to barbecue foods kept in the refrigerator or freezer on the spur of the moment. When preparing or storing marinades or sauces, be sure the container is not made of aluminum, as it tends to impart a somewhat "metallic" taste to the ingredients. It is far better to prepare the marinades and sauces (and to marinate also) in a glass, pottery, or ceramic container. For some reason, stainless steel containers apparently do not act in the same fashion as does aluminum, and they may therefore be used without imparting an "off-taste."

Beer Marinade

¼ cup olive oil
1½ cups beer
 1 teaspoon salt
½ teaspoon ground black
    pepper

1 teaspoon dry mustard
1 clove garlic, minced

Mix all ingredients. Use as a marinade for pork, beef, shellfish, or game.
Yields about 1¾ cups.

Onion Marinade (Greek)

½ cup olive oil
¼ cup lemon juice
2 cups diced onions
2 teaspoons oregano
¾ cup peeled, diced
    tomatoes

2 teaspoons salt
¾ teaspoon freshly ground
    black pepper
2 bay leaves, crumbled

Combine all ingredients in an electric blender container. Blend until smooth. Use for marinating lamb or beef cubes.

This sauce may also be used as marinade for leg of lamb. Marinate the meat for 3 hours at room temperature or overnight in the refrigerator. Turn and baste the meat several times.

Yields about 3 cups.

Yogurt Marinade (Turkish)

2 cups unflavored yogurt
1 cup grated onions
2 teaspoons salt
¾ teaspoon freshly ground black pepper

Mix all ingredients. Use as marinade for lamb kabobs. Sprinkle meat with cinnamon before cooking, if desired.

Yields 3 cups.

White Wine Marinade, Italian Style

1 cup dry white wine
½ cup olive oil
1 clove garlic, minced
2 tablespoons wine vinegar
½ cup grated onion
1 teaspoon salt
½ teaspoon freshly ground black pepper
½ teaspoon rosemary
½ teaspoon thyme

Mix all ingredients. Use an an overnight marinade for chicken, lamb, or pork. Drain meat before cooking and brush with marinade several times while meat is cooking.

Yields 2 cups.

African Peanut Sauce for Grilled Steak

3 tablespoons olive oil
1 cup chopped onions
½ cup chopped green
  peppers
1 cup chopped tomatoes
1½ teaspoons salt

Dash Tabasco
1 teaspoon Spanish paprika
1 cup ground peanuts
1½ cups beef broth
¼ cup heavy cream

Heat oil in a skillet; sauté onions and green peppers 5 minutes. Add tomatoes, salt, Tabasco, and paprika; cook over low heat 5 minutes. Mix in peanuts and broth; cook 30 minutes. Stir in cream; taste for seasoning. Serve with grilled steak.

Yields about 2½ cups.

Barbecue Sauce, Greek Style

2 cups dry red wine
¾ cup lemon juice
½ cup minced onions
2 cloves garlic, minced
¼ cup chopped parsley
¼ cup chopped celery
  leaves

2 teaspoons salt
½ teaspoon freshly ground
  black pepper
1 teaspoon oregano

Combine all ingredients in a bowl. Use as an overnight marinade for beef. Drain the meat, and use the marinade to baste while cooking or for basting while grilling.

Yields enough for 4 pounds of meat.

Barbecue Sauce, Mexican Style

½ cup olive oil
1 cup chopped onions
1 clove garlic, minced
1 20-ounce can tomatoes
1½ teaspoons salt

Dash cayenne pepper
2 tablespoons chili
   powder
¼ cup cider vinegar

Heat 2 tablespoons of oil in a saucepan. Add the onions and sauté until browned. Add garlic, tomatoes, salt, pepper, chili powder, and remaining oil. Bring to a boil and cook over low heat 20 minutes. Add vinegar and cook an additional 10 minutes.
Use as a basting sauce for chicken, pork, or beef.
Yields about 2¼ cups.

Spicy Barbecue Sauce, Panama Style

4 cups ketchup
½ cup prepared mustard
½ cup cider vinegar
½ cup Worcestershire
   sauce
2 teaspoons Tabasco

½ cup horseradish
2 teaspoons salt
1 teaspoon freshly ground
   black pepper
1 teaspoon garlic, minced
1 teaspoon sage

Combine all ingredients in a saucepan; bring to a boil. Use for basting spareribs, pork, or hamburgers.
Yields about 5 cups.

Barbecue Sauce, Portuguese Style

1 cup dry sherry
¼ cup olive oil
¾ cup minced onions
1 clove garlic, minced
1½ teaspoons salt

½ teaspoon freshly ground
    black pepper
½ teaspoon crushed
    tarragon

Mix all ingredients in a saucepan. Bring to a boil, and cook over low heat 5 minutes. Use for basting poultry on grill or spit.

Yields about 1¾ cups.

Barbecue Sauce, Texas Style

2 tablespoons vegetable oil
1 cup minced onions
2 cloves garlic, minced
½ cup finely chopped
    green pepper
½ cup grated carrots
2 cups chili sauce
1 cup water

¾ cup cider vinegar
2 teaspoons salt
2 tablespoons
    Worcestershire sauce
¼ teaspoon Tabasco
1 tablespoon bottled liquid
    smoke

Heat oil in saucepan; sauté onions, garlic, green pepper, and carrots for 5 minutes. Mix all remaining ingredients. Bring to a boil and cook over low heat 30 minutes, stirring several times. This mixture may be used to baste meats, poultry, or fish, or as a sauce.

Yields about 4 cups.

Barbecue Sauce, West Indian Style

1 pound tomatoes, peeled
and chopped
1 pound white onions,
peeled and chopped
½ teaspoon dried red
pepper flakes

3 cloves garlic, minced
2 whole cloves
6 black peppercorns
2 teaspoons salt
¼ cup lime or lemon juice
Cider vinegar

Combine all ingredients except vinegar in a sterile, 16-ounce jar. Pack the mixture down firmly, then fill with cider vinegar. Cover tightly and let stand 1 week. Use for fish, poultry, or meat.

Yields 1 pint.

Ginger Barbecue Sauce

2 cups ginger marmalade

¾ cup dry sherry

Heat marmalade and sherry in a small saucepan; mix until well blended. If a smoother sauce is desired, combine in blender.

Use for basting ham, duck, or pork.

Yields about 2 cups.

Saté Sauce (Indonesian)

1 large onion
1 cup vegetable oil
¼ pound (1 stick) butter
1 cup soy sauce

¼ cup lemon juice
½ teaspoon cayenne
pepper

Peel and quarter onion. Cut each quarter into paper-thin slices. Heat oil in a skillet until it bubbles. Add onions and fry them until crisp and golden brown. Drain on paper towels.

Melt butter in a saucepan; add soy sauce, lemon juice, and cayenne pepper. Bring to a boil and cook, covered, over low heat 5 minutes. Pour into a heatproof sauceboat and sprinkle fried onions on top.

Yields about 1½ cups.

Index

Catalog

If you are interested in a list of fine Paperback
books, covering a wide range of subjects
and interests, send your name and address,
requesting your free catalog, to:

McGraw-Hill Paperbacks
1221 Avenue of Americas
New York, N.Y. 10020